The Everyday Patriot

Other books by Tom Morris include:

NonFiction

Making Sense of It All
God and the Philosophers
True Success: A New Philosophy of Excellence
If Aristotle Ran General Motors
The Art of Achievement
Philosophy for Dummies
The Stoic Art of Living
Superheroes and Philosophy
If Harry Potter Ran General Electric
Socrates in Silicon Valley
Plato's Lemonade Stand

Fiction

The Oasis Within
The Golden Palace
The Stone of Giza
The Viper and the Storm
The King and Prince
The Mysterious Village
The Magic Ring
The Ancient Scroll

TOM MORRIS

Author of the National Bestsellers
If Aristotle Ran General Motors
If Harry Potter Ran General Electric

THE EVERYDAY PATRIOT

How To Be A
Great American Now

A Call To Action For Our Time

Wisdom/Work
Published by Wisdom Work
TomVMorris.com

Published 2022

Copyright © 2022, Tom Morris

ISBN 978-1-7377227-2-4

Printed in the United States of America

Set in Adobe Garamond Pro
Designed by Abigail Chiaramonte
Cover Concept by Sara Morris

*"We have too many high sounding words,
and too few actions that correspond to them."*

Abigail Adams (1744-1818)

To all the everyday patriots
of the present day.
May our numbers increase.

Contents

Preface

IF YOU'VE EVER WATCHED THE POPULAR AND ENTERTAINING *Antiques Road Show* on PBS, you've likely seen people who snagged something at a yard sale for four dollars or maybe twenty, and they brought it to the show curious about what it is and whether they got a good deal. We then get to see them discover it's really worth thousands of dollars, or tens of thousands, or even more. I envy those people. Why am I not one of them? I once spent thirty dollars at a yard sale on something I really wanted and, when I got my coveted item home, my wife explained to me that it was likely worth about five.

This book was inspired by the ultimate yard sale purchase of a cheap framed picture for exactly four dollars that turned out to have an original copy of the Declaration of Independence hidden away inside it. You may have heard about it. A friend of mine then bought the cherished document that had been printed in 1776 as one of several to be carried around the colonies and read aloud in public places. Going far beyond *Antiques Road Show* prices, he actually paid eight million dollars for it at a public auction. He wanted to send it across America for people to be able to see what he thought of as "the nation's birth certificate." He had called to tell me about his ideas for this new purchase, and our talk that day inspired me to look again, more closely than ever before, at the founding manifesto for our nation's life. I was amazed right away by a thought of how its biggest ideas could spark a positive revolution again in our own time, in our attitudes and actions in support of our communities and the nation. I'll tell you more about the story of that historic document's purchase and how it led to this book a little later. I want to show in these pages how our most crucial founding values and the ideals associated with them that are expressed and intimated in the Declaration of Independence can potentially bring us together in new ways around the great nation-building project we need to do for our land in every generation. These ideas are vitally important, and I hope they will move you as much as they have me.

I chose the phrase "The Everyday Patriot" as the title of this book for several reasons. The word 'patriotism' and its derivative 'patriot' have unfortunately become controversial in our time, due primarily to being misused. I've devoted my life as a philosopher to reclaiming certain concepts like success, happiness, wisdom, and virtue from various modern misunderstandings and bringing them back to their ancient and best meanings for our present and future. I hope to do that now with the idea of patriotism. The Oxford English Dictionary defines 'patriot' as "One who defends or is zealous for his country's prosperity, freedom, or rights." And of course zeal is just energetic passion. Merriam-Webster says, simply, "love for or devotion to one's country." The roots of the word trace back to the late sixteenth century French 'Compatriote,' that in turn derived from the fifteenth century 'Patriote,' itself having much older roots in a sixth century Latin term for "fellow-countryman" and even older Latin and Greek words for "homeland," or "fatherland," or "motherland." By the eighteenth century, patriotism was largely thought of within our shores as an attitude and commitment devoted to the broadest safety and wellbeing of our fellow citizens in our joint project of living and working together in this land.

I think of patriotism at its core as being a loyalty and love for our nation that wishes it the best and works toward that goal in everyday ways on a local scale where we live, in our neighborhoods, workplaces, and broader communities. As I'll explain later on, proper patriotism is an inner determination and commitment to act for the good of our country and all who live within it, together with an outer pattern of ongoing action that delivers real value to the larger world. It's a beneficial involvement in the life of our nation, with a lively concern for what we can contribute beyond its borders, in making our positive difference to the common good on however small or great a scale. It's supportive and creative. Patriotism is not by nature inherently adversarial at all. It's about being our best together or, as the ancient philosophers would say, it's a commitment to individual and community flourishing in all ways throughout our own nation, and then reaching across the globe with encouragement and friendship. We need to renew and embrace this important concept, understood aright, for our time and our lives at the present moment. It's one of the most important challenges and opportunities we face. If we can get it right, we can deal much better with every other challenge that confronts us.

But there are major obstacles to attaining this sort of spirit across the land. And they need to be mentioned. There was a delightful little book entitled *The Great Divorce* written in England during the last terrible days of World War II and published in 1945 by C.S. Lewis, a famous professor of English Literature at Oxford University. It told a fantastical story about a bus trip from hell to heaven. The day trippers whose choices in this life had landed them in a sad and unpleasant domain were given this unexpected excursion to let them look around heaven and see what alternative paths could lead to instead. At the end of the trip, they were given the opportunity to let go of whatever besetting sin had excluded them from this utterly wonderful place they were visiting, and then as a result stay in paradise. If they could just give up their hatreds and idolatries, their favored forms of bitterness, their resentments and attitudes of dismissiveness and even rage toward other human beings, they would be welcomed into the arms of their loving creator and allowed an enjoyment of bliss forever. But then oddly, we see these individuals unable to let go of their pet hostility, grievance, or warped attachment for the sake of a much greater existence. Many of them find themselves with the attitude of John Milton's character Satan in Paradise Lost, who says, "Evil, be thou my good!" They've accepted false goods, poisonous inner feelings, and orientations that have brought them a poor counterfeit of happiness based on a mistaken sense of self-righteousness and superiority to others. They can't manage to release this in order to enter a great community of true happiness and fellowship that's openly available to them.

This depiction of human tendencies that Lewis so brilliantly gave us characterizes far too many of us today across our nation in relation to our highest worldly possibilities of living well together. We're angry about something and ill disposed to others who don't share our views. We marinate in irritation or even fury as we blame "those people" for our troubles. And this has created a terrible unhealthiness in our nation that has to be overcome quickly and decisively by as many of us as possible. There are serious problems we need to solve, and if we don't address them soon and create more positive ways forward for our collective endeavor here in America, we may lose the chance to do so at all. But that will require lots of us coming together in a committed mindset that wants to take healthy and crucial actions at all levels of our national life. We need to release whatever is holding us back, let go of the negativities that have sadly come to define our time, and enter into a new culture of positive patriotism throughout the land that's based on the founding values and ideals of our distinctive nation. That's what this book is all about, and how to do it together.

Introduction

THE CALL OF OUR TIME

NOW IS OUR TIME. THIS IS OUR MOMENT. We need to step up to make a difference. And we can. The American adventure of freedom, equality, and justice is in our hands. It may sound like too much to say that even the fate of the earth may hinge on what we do now, but it's no exaggeration at all. The challenges we face are many and momentous, and as a result, the opportunities we have are immense. The future of our nation and, indirectly of humankind, turns on how we act now as the citizens of our highly visible democracy and the pioneers in our day for living its stated values in the world.

It's a good time for a new understanding of patriotism in America, inspired by our oldest ideals. We also need a broader, deeper, and more expansive idea of citizenship connected with it. A powerful vision for what it means to be a patriotic citizen in our day can energize and guide us into the future. Our nation can't wait any longer. Neither can the world. The time has come for a renewed clarity about who we are and what we can do together. The call of our day demands some important new attitudes and vital new actions. We're at a watershed moment on which so much turns.

In The United States of America, we're citizens of what is in many ways the most distinctive nation in history. It's an enterprise deliberately built on visionary ideas that can offer the greatest real potential for political freedom and personal growth. And yet in recent years, we've been in danger of forgetting this. Many of us have lost sight of what our citizenship should mean within the context of such a creative political adventure. We've been mainly asleep to our personal responsibilities as Americans for far too long. And sleepwalkers can't do great things. In the past few decades, the basic idea of citizenship has sadly become little more than a thin abstraction for many of us, a biographical detail that's only sporadically thought of as relevant to our ongoing lives.

Most of us pay our taxes and use the US Postal Service, and we might vote in national or local elections. On Memorial Day or the Fourth of July, we could have a special cookout with family and friends and perhaps think for a moment about our country's past, and then in the big midsummer celebration watch a few fireworks. As individuals, we may even feel an inner stirring when we hear "America The Beautiful," the national anthem, or "God Bless America." Various of our public holidays might make us pause for a few moments of reflection and gratitude. We could also have an American flag somewhere, or a related bumper sticker on the family car or truck. But few of us move through a typical day thinking of ourselves as American citizens in any robust and important sense. Too many of us have lost our sense of the immediacy and importance of our great national affiliation and what it should mean in our lives.

ↅ

It is a known fact in human nature that its affections are commonly weak in proportion to the distance or diffusiveness of the object.
Alexander Hamilton

ↅ

We normally think of ourselves as belonging to a particular family, working at a specific place, doing a certain job, and being part of a special circle of friends. We may even feel some sense of identity in connection with our neighborhood, city, county, or state, but for the most part, I suspect, not to the extent that many once did. Most of us have somehow managed to lose an important sense of connection with each other within and across our varied communities as the twentieth century came to a close and a new millennium began. We're mobile. We're global. We're nonlocal. We generally seem to have much less of an identification with our physical areas of residence—our geographic locations of neighborhood, town, state, and nation—than ever before. And, in reference to the country as a whole, the fundamental fact of our national citizenship has gradually moved to the outer periphery of our hearts and minds. Too many of us have lost any sense of personal investment and emotional ownership in our local communities. And far too great a number of us have ceased to feel any real sense of personal creative participation in the collaborative effort that is our nation. This is not as it should be.

ఌ
Man was born not for himself alone,
but for his country.
Plato
ఌ

And yet, in the midst of what are in many ways tremendously difficult and challenging times, there is some good news about our national spirit across America now. People are beginning to wake up and take to the streets to march for their highest values. Many of us sense a need for change. The conditions required for a healthy democracy have been eroding around us. People suffer in too many needless ways. A visceral reaction against corruption in high places and across important institutions has sparked the beginning of a long overdue transformation of attitudes around the nation toward our life together. We're sensing we need to get more involved and take action. I'm also seeing the spread of a deep disappointment with the incivility and even rage in public political discourse, and this has caused many to search for a better way to interact with those around us who believe, say, and feel different things.

Several people in public life have sought in recent years to remind us that the change we want is ultimately up to us, citing Gandhi's important message long ago that we must be the change we want to see in the world. The sad truth is that we have largely failed to be that positive change. We have elected or allowed people to stay in power who have blocked and constrained the improvement of our national life in almost every way possible. Racism has disguised itself in a hundred ways and worked under devious false flags to undermine what should be. Narrow financial interests have dangerously distorted public policy. Anger has corroded our national discourse.

၅

The future is in our hands.
The Dalai Lama

၅

There are always a few prominent individuals who seek to unite us around our highest common values. But others who profit from division will not rest, and typically use every tool at their command to thwart any good that might be done. As we've all seen in the recent past, destructive media have arisen and multiplied from the age-old desire for money and power and, disguising themselves as patriotic voices, their personalities have sought to dismantle the greatness of the nation while loudly pretending to do the opposite.

There's an old adage: Hurt people hurt people. Damaged egos can blithely destroy for the sake of their own felt needs. Too many injured souls seek political office or to have a public political voice for the personal power, fame, and wealth it can bring, rather than to serve the greater good.

But the rest of us want something more and better for our country, for our own sense of ourselves as Americans, and for our role in the world. And it's beginning to look like a clear majority of us are ready for it now. The exciting thing is that it is indeed up to us, each of us, to make our needed transformative change together.

We have a chance at this moment to rethink our citizenship together, redefine our sense of patriotism in a strongly positive way, and renew the great adventure that our founders began for our benefit long ago. Patriotism itself has of course become a distorted and misunderstood idea among many, but I want to introduce a new sense of it that's actually an old understanding, and one that's urgently needed in our day. We're living at a time when we need a revival of active, grassroots democracy across the land. And we can make it happen. We can launch a new era for our nation with our attitudes and actions each day, as we make creative contributions to our social and political environment, spurred on by the encouragement that we're not acting alone.

We've realized for many years that the physical infrastructure of our nation requires extended attention. We clearly need to do a great deal of work on our roads, bridges, sewers, water supplies, harbors, mass transit systems, and electric grid, as well as providing secure and reliable high speed internet availability for all. But what's not as widely recognized is that there is a social infrastructure for our democracy that needs just as much attention and work. It involves active community groups that enrich local life, broad-based volunteer organizations focused on the health of the nation, far thinking business leaders concerned with the greater good, and multitudes of energized individuals on fire with a lively sense of our personal responsibilities as citizens. It's up to us now to rejuvenate this vital democratic infrastructure, retool our attitudes as Americans, and revive a robust understanding of proper patriotism that's healthy and positive for our time. A house or car needs regular maintenance and care. So does our common home.

༄

Let's take the opportunity this day has given us.
Horace

༄

We are at a moment when necessity has sparked possibility. Very different visions of the future that can lie ahead of us have begun to incite a new wave of conviction and public passion throughout the land. In his classic book, *Democracy in America*, published as two volumes in the years 1835 and 1840, respectively, the deeply insightful French analyst of our nation, Alexis de Tocqueville, suggested that big goals can rouse great passions, and that whenever such focused passions spread broadly enough through the population, major things can happen. When the passions are wise, the results can be dramatic and good. He wrote that, "In a great republic, political passions become irresistible not only because the object they pursue is immense, but also because millions of men feel them in the same manner and at the same moment." The goals of renewing America, returning to the ideals of our founders, and restoring our proper place of leadership in the world are in fact big aspirations of the sort that Tocqueville saw as distinctly powerful. And they're beginning to arouse great passion in millions of us. So now, we have a rare opportunity to do something important in our day.

An Invitation

I WANT TO ENCOURAGE YOU TO PARTICIPATE PERSONALLY IN this new chance for renewal, and to do so thoughtfully and intelligently, with a deep understanding of everything that's on the line. We clearly stand at a new and dangerous crossroads in history. As Americans, we can be a shining example or a discouraging object lesson to the rest of the world. The latter result has become an increasingly serious threat, but because of it, we can be sparked into the positive action we need.

It's the dream of many now that we can come alive with a new understanding of ourselves as both Americans and world citizens, and that with a fresh enthusiasm for our potential role in the progress of humanity, we'll be spurred on to get busy with an everyday patriotism that can make a huge positive difference for us all. That's what I want this little book to help you ponder and accomplish in some small way. I hope to persuade or at least to remind you that an engaged citizenship and a sense of patriotic care aren't exclusively the concern of a few distant, rare leaders who steer the ship of state, and they're not just the business of occasional heroes who rise up and respond to dramatic events in ways that inspire us all. The call to action we're hearing now isn't merely for the few.

It's for all of us. It's meant to be an important task for each of us throughout the everyday adventures of our lives. The vision of our founders was that "we the people" would lead our nation together into the bright future we all deserve.

Here is the key: Citizenship isn't just a legal status; it's a moral calling. And patriotism isn't just a feeling. It's an equally moral commitment that can be a powerful impetus for making our neighborhoods, our nation, and our world a better place. It is our duty, and can be an important part of our joy. When we have a deeper and richer sense of ourselves as Americans, we can do great things together.

გ

Our country is the common parent of all.
Cicero

გ

Our Problem and
Its Solution

THERE HAVE BEEN TIMES OF A STRONG, positive and widespread patriotic spirit in America rooted in our nation's founding promise and ideals. There have been stretches of our history when people felt intimately connected with their communities and our country around those ideals, despite our collective imperfections and even serious inconsistencies in living the values we espouse. We have had days of tremendous pride in our cities, states, and nation. When I was growing up in North Carolina in the now ancient fifties, I was taught as a little boy to declare, "I'm a Tar Heel Born, and a Tar Heel Bred, and when I Die I'll be Tar Heel Dead." Those words were part of a rousing homespun anthem of belonging and pride in my state. I deeply identified not only with my immediate family, our small house, and the people who lived along our recently paved street, but also with my hometown of Durham and even the broader reaches of our beautiful state. Our extended neighborhood was my playground. The Durham Bulls were my baseball team. I was a committed Carolina Tar Heel basketball fan. And I was a proud American. So were my friends. But as the years passed, I began to notice a change.

For many decades, we've lived in the most highly mobile society in all of history. People as a result, especially in recent years, have often felt less of a sense of place in which their lives are rooted and grow. Many of us typically have a more tenuous emotional attachment to our geographical region, state, and local area of residence, which may change every few years as we move from one job to another. As a result, we feel a diminished sense of community in our neighborhoods and towns. At the same time, we've become so busy in our various individual pursuits of work, love, acceptance, and success that the felt realities of any larger, overarching sense of national citizenship have also waned in our hectic lives.

While the basic idea of citizenship seems to have receded from the everyday awareness of so many Americans, the potentially more exalted idea of patriotism may have grown hollow for vast numbers of us as well. It's at once still a stubbornly attractive quality to at least many, and yet somehow, at the same time, it may seem almost quaint. It can easily come across nowadays as an old-fashioned idea, a nostalgic holdover from the eras of Paul Revere or Pearl Harbor. Some concerned critics even think of patriotism as a dangerous idea aligned with xenophobic, jingoistic, adversarial mindsets that have always been harmful, and are more threatening than ever before in our high tech and elaborately connected world. But a proper form of patriotism reflecting our highest values, a genuine and appropriate love for our home country, can be one of the most important and positive things in the world, as well as for the world.

In this short book, I want to make a statement about citizenship and patriotism in our day. I'll explain my own sense of what it means for any of us to be patriotic citizens in all the best ways, and then urge you to join me in launching into a personal plan of action as a result of this understanding. I want to help you think about what it takes to be an American citizen as an active and intentional response to the challenging political events of our day and the many other problems we face. I also want to help you come to a deep and yet simple view of what it means to be a great American now. It's time to settle for nothing less.

❧

He loves his country best who strives to make it best.
Robert G. Ingersoll

❧

The ancient philosopher Plato believed that for any republic to prosper, every citizen in the land must play a proper role. Aristotle later declared about the most basic political unit of his day, the *polis* or city-state, that, "A city is a partnership for living well." And this is an idea of great power. I think his insight applies at every level of our lives in contemporary America. A neighborhood should be thought of as a partnership for living well, and so should a town, and a state, and the nation. We are partners in a grand and vital enterprise. If we can come to see and live that partnership more deeply, each of us will be more likely to make our proper contribution to the human adventure.

I once enjoyed reading an insightful business book with the interesting title, *Perfecting a Piece of the World*. That phrase provides a solid hint about what we should pursue as citizens and patriotic Americans. It's a form of commitment to the nation we all can embrace. It simply involves daily attention and action. The everyday patriot is not often required to exhibit great courage or to accomplish anything monumental. The person I have in mind is typically just an individual who regularly works to improve his or her little piece of this nation, and in this way tries to perfect a piece of the world.

We need to reclaim the most fundamental, high concept of patriotism for our time and learn how to live it personally and together throughout our days. This idea of patriotism isn't about any sort of collective narcissism or self-righteous superiority. It's not us against the world. It doesn't focus on aggressive displays of symbolism or snappy slogans that go viral online. It's not a political weapon or a deceptive cloak for hidden motives. It isn't belligerently exclusionary. It's instead a positive and powerfully invitational approach to daily life. It's about healthy choices rooted in reliable knowledge. It's about taking action of the right sort.

‹›

Action is the proper fruit of knowledge.
Thomas Fuller

‹›

Ultimately, everyday patriotism is an ongoing commitment to regular action for the common good from which we all benefit. In this little book, we'll look at what it takes to be a suitably active citizen and an everyday patriot in our time. Then with a new and shared understanding, we can get moving in new ways together.

‹›

"What a long preamble," he said, "when I'm so keen to hear what
you're getting at!"
"All right," I said. "See if you think there's anything in what I say."
Glaucon and Socrates, sounding like Piglet and Pooh,
in Plato, Republic, *(432e-433a)*

‹›

The Everyday Patriot

LET'S DO A QUICK THOUGHT EXPERIMENT. If I asked you right now to name some great Americans, to create a list, what would you come up with right away? Whose names would immediately leap to mind? Would you think of such individuals as George Washington, Abraham Lincoln, Ben Franklin, Thomas Jefferson, John Adams, Patrick Henry, Betsy Ross, Susan B. Anthony, Eleanor Roosevelt, John F. Kennedy, or Martin Luther King, Jr.? Most people would come up with a list that at least started with names like these. In some circles, I might even hear names like James Madison, Dwight Eisenhower, Daniel Webster, Rosa Parks, John Lewis, Ralph Waldo Emerson, Henry David Thoreau, and Booker T. Washington. These are certainly all very accomplished individuals who did do great things for our nation. But notice something right away: they're all people in the past who are no longer living among us.

Here's the really important question: Where are the great Americans now, the great Americans of the present day? If we needed to go find some, where would we look?

I personally think they're all over the place. They're in New York City firehouses, police stations in Denver, and school rooms in Boston and Grand Rapids. They're working the docks in San

Francisco, staffing a senior center in Baltimore, volunteering at a hospital in Tulsa, commuting to work every day in Minneapolis, and building a good business in Austin. Some are plowing fields near Natchez or Des Moines, serving on the city council in Phoenix, helping the Boys and Girls Club of Wilmington, counseling a single mother in Fresno, and perhaps reading books aloud to children right now in Miami, Cleveland, South Bend, and Charleston, as well as in a vast number of other cities and small towns whose names you may never have heard, but where great things happen.

At least part of the answer to my question of where the great Americans are right now could possibly be that there are some in your town, in your neighborhood, and perhaps even in your own home. You yourself may one day get onto someone's list.

I can imagine that with any measure of normal humility, you might greet this particular suggestion with some good-natured skepticism. But maybe you shouldn't. After all, George Washington didn't begin life as a great American. He was once just a little boy in Virginia. And he had his flaws, like everybody else. Abraham Lincoln was a poor kid in the Midwest. Nobody could look at the little baby named Martin Luther King, Jr. and tell that he would one day make history and launch change across the land. None of these individuals started life as great Americans. They became great because of the choices they made and what they did as a result, because of their strong determination to make a difference, and all the many actions their attitudes produced.

ᴄ⁄ᴐ

He is great who confers the most benefits.
Ralph Waldo Emerson

ᴄ⁄ᴐ

It's been like that throughout the whole sweep of human history. Even the pinnacle of worldly greatness has always come from small beginnings. In ancient times, Alexander the Great had to start somewhere. When he was quite young, I suspect that to the casual glance he may have been just Alexander the Average, but he became great, or at least quite accomplished, through what he learned, how he grew, and what he chose to do. Sure, he had help. Aristotle taught him well. Of course, we won't all be world conquerors, but however modest we think our own beginnings to have been, we can make a difference for our nation and our world by doing the right little things, right where we are. That's the way it's been for all the greatest Americans of the past. They started out basically like you and I. They learned from those who had gone before them. And at some point they decided as individuals to take action and make a difference, if even in apparently small ways. But as their examples show, when you do the little things well, you sometimes end up with big results. And the biggest results always arise from our cumulative impact, each of us doing what we can with what we have, where we are.

Our idea of greatness itself needs to be a little greater, both broader and deeper. Greatness doesn't have to involve money, fame, or power, exceptional talent or high status, or any form of national or global notice. But it does have to produce true benefits for the good of others. And that's something we're all capable of accomplishing in our lives with our time, attention, and energies. Our English word 'great' comes from older roots that meant, among other things, big, abundant, or important, and it's connected with the verb 'greaten' that meant to enlarge or increase. Our lives can be great, in the sense of inwardly rich, abundant, and enlarging on whatever geographical or social scale we live.

&

There is no greatness where there is no simplicity,
goodness and truth.
Leo Tolstoy

&

I've known a great man who was a janitor. He enlarged the job. It never constrained or diminished him. He acted authentically and greatly where he was by being deeply who he was. He touched lives. The benefits he conferred were many. By the time I got to work in the morning as a professor at a great university, he had already absorbed the news of the day and developed a spin on world events that was amazing to me as he greeted me and we talked. His cheerfulness raised spirits. He inspired people to action. He was an example to me of a great American. He made a positive difference every day.

How about you? Can you enlarge the borders of your life and your work even a little, and more intentionally make your difference in a new way? From small acts of kindness that heal and encourage, to volunteer initiatives on a community-wide scale, there are things that each of us can do to be active citizens and great Americans wherever we might live, and however occupied we otherwise might be.

The Greatness
that Counts

You don't have to get your picture into the history books to be a great American. You don't need to stride across a world stage leading huge enterprises, rousing the multitudes, or making the news. It's not necessary to be rich, photogenic, immensely talented, or well connected. You don't have to be a world-class genius or celebrated hero. You just have to decide as an individual to take action and make a difference for the good of others as well as yourself. Pay attention to what's needed around you. Give something of yourself. Do a little more for your community. Help some of your neighbors. Use your talents. Offer your time. Make a personal contribution for good. Greatness can indeed result.

&

To be an American is of itself almost
a moral condition, an education, and a career.
George Santayana

&

I want my life to make a difference. I bet you do too. That's why we're here. We're born not just to go through the motions, take up space, do work we may not like, eat, shop, sleep, wander through life, complain a bit, and die. We're in this world because we all have something to offer, something that in its own way and on its own scale can genuinely be great. There's a purpose, and even a mission, for each of us.

In my work, I'm a philosopher. That may sound like an odd or pretentious job description, but it isn't. I'm not a Plato or Aristotle, or even a Ralph Waldo Emerson. But my job is wisdom—finding, living, and sharing it. And where I am right now in my life of discovering, embracing, and spreading wisdom could not have been predicted from my start in the world. I grew up in a tiny rented house, surrounded by money troubles. I'm the first person in my family to go to college, and with an unquenchable thirst for education, I went on to graduate school. We weren't able to afford any of it, but thanks to generous scholarships and the help of friends and family, I got to attend the University of North Carolina for a first degree, and then go on to Yale for several more.

I had the great experience of teaching at The University of Notre Dame for fifteen years, and then launched out in a new adventure to serve in a different way, to travel the nation as a public philosopher, talking with people everywhere about what the great thinkers of the past discovered for our quest of personal success, organizational excellence, and happiness in life. One thing I've learned in the process is that our success should never be measured in dollars, celebrity, or cultural power. It's all too often judged in precisely these terms, but we shouldn't confuse the occasional trappings of success with what is really its heart. True success is more a matter of who we are, what we do with our talents and opportunities, and the positive impact we have on other people, however small it might seem. It's about our individual contribution to the greater good, and the legacy we leave. It's the positive difference we make, each in our own way.

☙

We cannot insure success, but we can deserve it.
John Adams

☙

We can both deserve success and attain it *as citizens*, and not just in our careers and personal lives. I see authentic personal success as always tied in with forms of caring. The moral calling of citizenship is a duty to care. It's a personal responsibility to pay attention to the needs around us and partner up with others to make a difference sparked by those needs. It's an obligation to take an interest in making our communities and our nation a little better, from wherever we're positioned. Am I improving my community and country through my actions or not? Am I promoting harmony and health, and working for the welfare of others as well as myself? Am I successfully answering the call of citizenship through my daily decisions at work and in my personal time? Are you?

☙

We all have ability. The difference is how we use it.
Stevie Wonder

☙

My parents were great Americans, despite their many problems. They weren't rich or famous or powerful, but they were deeply successful as citizens: they made a difference in their communities and in our nation for good. My mother was a Rosie the Riveter during the Second World War at Martin Aircraft in Baltimore, standing for long stretches up on a platform with her rivet gun, attaching center section metal to military planes being sent overseas. She worked hard, and wouldn't let anyone get away with shoddy results. She'd catch any sloppy work and say, "Our boys' lives depend on this plane! Do it right or don't do it at all." She was a great American in her own way.

My father at that time was just off the farm, in his late teens and early twenties, helping to design and build those airplanes. He had mastered the work demands of every department at Martin Aircraft. The company's leadership told the War Department that he shouldn't be drafted into military duty but stay on the job because he knew as much about airplane design at the age of twenty as anyone else in America. He was needed where he was. The government official who reviewed his case replied that a young man his age could not possibly know that much, and so he ended up carrying a rifle in the South Pacific, serving the country any way he could. In the process, he lost his innocence, his best friend, and his innate inner peace, but he never lost his determination to make a difference for his fellow citizens and our nation. I often saw him go to extraordinary lengths in later years to help people newly arrived on our shores to get their start and live the American dream with their families. My dad was a great American too.

Many of us can report the same thing about our parents or grandparents and older aunts and uncles. They served this country well in many ways. They served their communities. They believed in our nation. They lived its values day-to-day. They made sacrifices. They took action. They did something good and made a difference.

ↄ

There is no power on earth that can neutralize
the influence of a high, simple, and useful life.
Booker T. Washington

ↄ

Others among us don't have ancestors who lived here for generations and long worked for our national good. They might represent a first generation on our shores, and they now seek to set this sort of example for those who will come after them. They get to begin the American experience for perhaps generations yet to come. Their children and grandchildren can then speak well of what they did now to make our joint enterprise of America better. Those of us are blessed who can speak this way already about so many of our forebears who've labored through the years to make this place on earth a good home. They gave us an example, and in many ways a country better than they found it, through the best things they did. But here's the question for all of us today: Are our children and future generations indeed going to be able to say the same things about us? Will they one day come to think of us as among the great Americans in our time? Will they thank us for our efforts? We can give them something to be proud of, too, but only if we take the right actions and make the right difference with our lives that we're capable of making.

And that's the problem. Life isn't a spectator sport, and neither is a proper patriotism. Citizenship isn't meant to be a passive fact. You don't serve your country well by just doing your job, minding your own business, and biding your time. You have to get off the bench and into the game. You're needed. I'm needed. If we can figure out how to take action where we are for the sake of our country, perhaps just in little ways, day-to-day, we can make a positive difference, and potentially for a long time to come.

America is a garden of possibilities. Don't be a weed. And don't even be a prize petunia. We all need to be active, creative gardeners with whatever small plot of soil has been committed to our care. And while we're at it, why shouldn't we seek to be among the truly great gardeners of our time? We need to get busy and tend the amazing, fertile, and lush garden we've been given, and we'd better get to it now. It's being buffeted and stressed by things that threaten its survival. Its future depends on us. And our own future depends on what we do for the greater good, both in it and with it, in however small a way every day.

☙

All gardeners live in beautiful places because they make them so.
Joseph Joubert

☙

I love this image for patriotism. Care for your garden. Make your garden great. Grow your plants well. Help your neighbors. Share. Flourish together. Notice that it's an interesting implication of the metaphor that great gardeners don't typically fight each other. They work the ground and produce good things. If I like peas and my neighbor prefers potatoes, that doesn't make us opponents or enemies. In fact it's our varied interests that may lead to a more diverse and potentially more beautiful and useful garden. A proper variety makes for a stronger form of health that's a benefit for all.

The Patriotic Spirit

SEVERAL YEARS AGO, my wife and I placed an American flag outside our house on the Fourth of July for the first time. I'm a little embarrassed to admit that we had never done this before. But in the past I've never been big on what I thought of as standard, popular displays of symbolism, simply because they can so easily become empty gestures. And yet, more recently, I started to rethink this a bit. So my family put our first flag in the front. And actually, we put out seventeen flags. "Why seventeen?" you may wonder. We ran out of room and flags.

But of course, displaying small flags in the yard is never enough. Putting a bumper sticker on the car doesn't do the work. I could wear a little American flag pin every time I leave the house, but that alone won't benefit the nation either. I need to figure out how to use my particular talents and spend a little bit of my limited personal time to take some real action and make a difference for our country. It might just be some small new way of getting more involved in my community that could end up generating big results. I'll share some great examples of this. The substance of patriotism is a special kind of love for our country, starting in our homes, neighborhoods, cities, counties, and states, and moving outward. It's a form of caring in action. It's my job as a patriotic citizen to figure out what I can do for the greater good, and then get busy doing it.

❧

The test of any man lies in action.
Pindar

❧

You need to figure out what you can do too. And we're going to talk about that. Our classic symbols of patriotism are fine. They are meant to represent the centuries and generations that have gone into creating and tending this garden of a nation. They're not to be coopted by those who hate gardens or seek to tear up what others have worked hard to plant. As positive symbols of a great mindset, they're ours to use with pride. But the time has come when we all need the real thing as well, the substance beyond the symbol, and in an ongoing way. Symbolism properly expresses reality. Without the practical reality of patriotic care and concern for our nation, even in its smallest parts, our finest symbols would indeed become empty gestures in our lives. And that means we need to invest some dedicated action into what they represent.

Here's the problem. We engage in constructive action only with motivation, but for a long time in America, it seems that many of us have lacked motivation for a full, robust, active sense of patriotic citizenship. In the Bible, the book of Proverbs says, "Without a vision, people perish." It seems that we've been without a compelling vision for our role as Americans for far too long. Most of us have had no big, animating conception of our life together in our families, neighborhoods, towns, nation, and world. As a result, people perish. We have habits and routines and, with heads down, we make it through the day. But we're missing something important. Only a powerful and proper vision for our lives as individuals among others in our communities, and a broader vision for what being an American really means, can motivate us to initiate the sort of actions we need to take every day in order to make the needed difference in our time.

The patriotic spirit can rise and fall in the life of an individual, and in the life of a nation. My own personal history illustrates this well. I grew up with a strongly positive view of this country and its potential. I've always been proud to be an American, and as a young child I thought of myself as a part of a big extended national family that embraced me as an individual. I can remember that in those years I felt I was somehow directly connected to our national government, thinking that it was in some very personal sense mine, and that our nation's leaders were concerned about kids like me.

When President John F. Kennedy was in office and I was a student in elementary school, I occasionally lay on the floor of our little four-room house and drew cartoons for the president's children, Caroline and John-John. One day, I put a few of those sketches into an envelope and addressed it to The White House, Washington, DC. My parents seemed to think this was the most natural thing in the world. They stuck on some stamps and dropped my little gift for the First Family into the mailbox.

Weeks later, a beautiful, crisp white envelope arrived by return mail. In the upper left corner, in bright blue ink, it said "The White House." I remember holding it in my hands and feeling very important and quite excited, but not in the least surprised. I opened it carefully and read a nice note from Mrs. Kennedy's Social Secretary and Chief of Staff, Letitia Baldridge, thanking me for the drawings and telling me how much Caroline and John-John had enjoyed them, and that Mrs. Kennedy wanted to let me know she appreciated my kindness in sending them. In America, I was convinced, every child counts. Each of us is genuinely important to our nation. And we can each do something that makes a difference, whatever our age and circumstances might be.

๛

Every man feels instinctively that all the beautiful sentiments
In the world weigh less than a single lovely action.
J.R. Lowell

๛

In my younger years, I was sufficiently sheltered from many of the challenges of the world and our nation that I was not aware of our collective flaws, our inherited problems, and how often we fail to live up to our founding ideals. But as I eventually learned these things, it didn't diminish my love for my country at all, and rather instilled in me a sense of how much work we have yet to do to bring our values more consistently into practice. It's the human condition. Our ideals typically outstrip our performance, and more work is needed for improvement. It's good to have such ideals precisely to give us direction and encourage us to grow and get better.

๛

We have advanced far enough to say that democracy
is a way of life. We have yet to realize that
it is a way of personal life and one which provides
a moral standard for personal conduct.
John Dewey

๛

A few years after my small artistic gift to the president's children, at the more mature age of twelve, I engaged in a classroom debate about one man's national political aims as if our little discussion would have a decisive impact on the upcoming election. Then in my twenties, while I was a student in graduate school working in two doctoral programs, I went door to door campaigning for a presidential candidate in the middle of what was perhaps some of the most hostile territory he faced. I even wrote a funny little country music campaign song in support of his efforts, a tune that I was always eager to perform for my bewildered Connecticut neighbors. The health of the nation mattered that much to me. And I credited the outcome of that election, at least in small part, to the cosmic impact of my doorstep orations and poorly crooned tunes.

From a young age, I had at least a basic sense of patriotism. In later life, as a philosopher, I've come to see things more deeply. I've learned that wisdom in general is about perspective and context, framing our experiences properly, seeing things in the right light, and appreciating the real connections events have. I've also come to understand that proper patriotism begins with perspective and context too. It means thinking within a broader horizon and seeing beyond our usual small, personal concerns. It involves having a bigger picture for our lives than a simple, nearsighted selfishness, and it means acting for the sake of a greater good, a good that eventually and wonderfully will favor the most enlightened self-interest that each of us appropriately has. I certainly hadn't thought through any of this intellectually as a child or in adolescence, but since even my early years, I have had at least a small inkling of it all.

I'm sharing with you this small bit of my background in patriotic thought and action not because I think I've had any noteworthy impact on the political fortunes of our country. I just want to indicate how much of an American I grew up feeling myself to be, and how naturally connected I felt with the larger context of our national governance and its electoral process. And yet even so, it wasn't long before the many concerns of marriage, career, fatherhood, daily work, and just the general busyness and exhaustion of adult life had eroded and displaced my sense of citizenship almost entirely.

In my growing maturity, I was capable of benefiting from and contributing to our national life in many more ways than when I was a young child, or even an older student, at least within the scope of my own community. But somehow, and for whatever reason, the thrill was gone. I began taking for granted the ebb and flow of daily life, everything that's convenient in this country, all that's available here, and the full range of what's possible because of our laws, structures, and freedoms. I completely forgot about the role that I should be playing in protecting and preserving the vital infrastructure of democracy that supported all the things about my life that I valued most.

Over time, I gradually lost my motivation to engage in acts of patriotic service at any level. I didn't follow the issues of the day. I didn't help any other national, state, or local campaigns, or express my political concerns to neighbors. I didn't do volunteer or charitable work in my community. I didn't even draw any more cartoons for presidential kids. I was too busy and distracted. I had forgotten the many moral requirements and the abundant possibilities of citizenship.

Hitting Bottom

MY PATRIOTISM BOTTOMED OUT. It's not that I ever had serious misgivings about the idea of patriotism itself. I never conflated it with a dangerously insidious nationalism, or thought of it as an ethically dubious preference for people who happen to live in proximity to me. I wasn't tempted to dismiss it as a "last refuge of scoundrels," or reject it as the sadly hypocritical pretense and disguise of demagogues and big-scale bullies. In fact, like a lot of other people, I came to think of patriotism as basically good-hearted and old-fashioned, but in the current age maybe a little over-the-top, like that aggressive school spirit shown by cheering too loudly for your high school team when they're already up by thirty points over a clearly weaker opponent. There came to be even something a little awkward feeling and almost embarrassing to me about overt and emotional displays of patriotic pride. It just all began to seem a little self-indulgently smug, perhaps unduly narrow, a bit naïve, overly sentimental, and a touch inexcusably self-congratulatory. I completely lost my grasp of what patriotism really means.

I lost touch with politics. I took a more casual attitude toward the news. And in very little time, I drifted into what I can only describe in retrospect as feeling almost completely disconnected from my larger community and nation. My little world had gradually shrunk that far. I'm more than a little ashamed to admit that in one election I can remember, I didn't even go to the trouble of voting. It was just a local election, I didn't know that much about any of the candidates, and on election day I was at first too busy and then, as a result of all I was doing, too tired to go and vote.

✑

The death of democracy is not likely to be an assassination from ambush. It will be a slow extinction from apathy, indifference, and undernourishment.
Robert Hutchins

✑

I was *too tired to vote*. Can you imagine that? Or do you know the feeling first hand? How can anyone be too tired to vote? I can understand being too tired to play another nine holes of golf after completing eighteen, feeling too tired to wash the car after running lots of errands and mowing the grass on a really hot day, being too tired for a pickup game of basketball after a long stretch of difficult hours at work, or feeling too tired to go out with friends late at night. But too tired to vote? Mark off your name here, walk over there, and then take a moment: Click, click, check, done. Too tired for that?

Of course, we are all masters of rationalizing. I wasn't really too tired. I was just unmotivated and very good at reinterpreting my behavior to make it all seem a little more justified. I had lost my sense of the importance of citizenship and its proper range of activities. As an American, I had lost my way. I didn't vote because somewhere deep in my heart I was thinking, "Why bother? What difference does it make?" I remember asking myself, "What's the use?" And I somehow almost managed to feel fine about what I was doing, or in this case not doing, although my choice wasn't fine at all.

cs

I find excuses for myself.
Horace

cs

Voter Apathy and Rationalization

WE HAVE A GREAT MANY EXCUSES AVAILABLE for not exercising our democratic right to vote. And some are admittedly clever. But none of them is any good. Remember, this is a right that people in other parts of the world have longed for and struggled hard to attain. It's a right that people in our own country have fought and died to secure and protect. In fact, there are far too many young men and women who continue to have to suffer and perish to safeguard it for the rest of us. And yet we stay home on Election Day and neglect our duty with a shrug and fundamentally bad excuses.

Just think for a second about all the utterly unoriginal things we sometimes say to rationalize our inertia: "My one vote won't make any difference." Or: "Politicians are all alike; it really doesn't matter." Or in cases where the candidates are obviously not alike and differ fundamentally in their views, we may have to get a little more subtle and argue: "These rival politicians are at bottom too much alike in one way: they're equally bound to special interests, powerful donors, conflicting constituencies, and of course their own party with all its baggage, while at the same time being constrained by the sheer weight of complex national and international structures that just won't allow that much room for change anyway. So, what's the real choice? Let's get a beer instead." Yeah. Ok. Why not go vote like it matters, like we mean it, and then have that beer?

I've even heard this: "My loving spouse, or good friend, or neighbor across the street will vote the other way and cancel out my vote. So we should both just stay home and call it even." There's a buddy system for apathy. Then, there is the apparently sensitive, distracted slacker claim: "I haven't had time to keep up on the issues and different positions at stake in this election. I really don't know the candidates well enough to make an informed decision. I'd do more harm than good by voting on this one. And I just don't have time right now to study up on it all and make a good decision."

In addition, many of us have at some point heard a supremely self-confident know-it-all report in a haughty voice of loud, clear, and assumed authority that no important major election has ever been settled by one or two or three votes, so he very rationally plans to do other things on election day, useful or enjoyable things, and he counsels us to follow his lead as well, since it won't really matter in the end whether we voted or not. Our little ballots can't make any difference at all. It's a pointless exercise. We're simply a bunch of pitiful, misguided idiots to think otherwise.

&

In the conduct of life we make use of deliberation
to justify ourselves in doing what we want to do.
W. Somerset Maugham

&

Here's the real truth. Every vote sends a message, whether it ever counts as the margin of electoral victory or not. And every vote contributes to the margin of victory, after all. Plus, if no two people are exactly alike, no two candidates are, either. We always have a choice. And it's neither enlightened nor rational to assume with a pretense of sophisticated fatalism that no particular candidate can make a distinctive difference while in office. Many have. And some manage to do so quite badly.

When any two people who disagree on politics stay home to keep from canceling each other's vote, they've canceled each other's voice. Their intentional absence from the process sends a vote of "no confidence" or at least of basic disinterest all by itself, whether that result is intended or not. Their action says, "This isn't worth the trouble of going down the street." It says that politicians can do whatever they want, however bad or even awful, and I won't bother to object with a mark on a piece of paper. It's a terrible and unjustified insult to the sacrifices made by good men and women and many children for over two hundred years, and it subtly erodes the foundations for future freedom and democracy in America, as well as throughout the world. It's never without a point in our nation to go and cast a vote. And it's one of the most destructive and cynical things anyone can do to seek to throw into doubt the integrity of the careful and well-guarded system we've constructed over time to try to make sure that each vote counts.

❧

At the bottom of all the tributes paid to democracy is the little man,
walking into the little booth, with a little pencil,
making a little cross on a little bit of paper—
no amount of rhetoric or voluminous discussion can possibly
diminish the overwhelming importance of this point.
Winston Churchill

❧

There are many people who just insist that they don't have time to get over to their local voting place and stand in line. If you ever hear something like this from family, friends, or neighbors, then tell them the story of Susan Scott-Ker and her husband, who as new citizens were excited about voting in their first presidential election. The problem was that a job transfer had put them in Bangalore, India, and their absentee ballot had not yet arrived when it was expected. They contacted the American Consulate, and no one was able to solve the problem. They even looked into getting an overnight courier service to help them. But possible bureaucratic snags made this inadvisable. In the end, they decided that the best thing to do was to come back to the U.S. and show up to vote in their local precinct. They got plane tickets and took off. Their schedule took them from Bangalore to New Delhi, to O'Hare, and finally to LaGuardia. They traveled 9,300 miles each way, and spent over $5,000 to be able to cast their votes for the candidates they thought would do the best job for the nation's future.

These two determined voters were later asked why they went to all that trouble to vote in New York State, where their favored candidates already had a comfortable lead in the polls, when they could have stayed in India and gotten the same election result. Ms. Scott-Ker said simply, "Then, you're relying on other people to do your job." And, as someone who clearly understands the nature of both real citizenship and true patriotism, she explained her commitment to action, however inconvenient, and her husband's, by saying simply that, "Apathy doesn't work in a democracy." It's a lesson and amazing example for us all. Even if I'm unwilling to cross the globe to vote, I can manage some way to make it across town. And so can you.

Democracy requires engagement. And that means involvement and action. Citizenship in a country like ours is both a privilege and a responsibility. We each have a job to do. And voting thoughtfully in all elections is an important part of it. We should take whatever steps are necessary in order to keep anything from interfering with our ability to do our job as American citizens. Then we need to do it well.

The very different "ignorance excuse" for not voting, if it's sincere, is indeed a real problem. But there are, in principle, two ways of dealing with it. Problems can be solved or, better yet, anticipated and avoided. If Election Day rolls around and you suddenly realize you know nothing about the candidates on the ballot, you do in fact have a problem. And it's one the rest of us share, because an ignorant or frivolous vote can in principle hurt us all, in however small a degree. But then again, any absence from the process diminishes the result overall in its own way.

I suppose that the person who lacks detailed electoral knowledge could solve his problem on the spot, at least to some extent, by texting or calling a friend for information, or else casting a straight party ballot, aligning himself with the basic approach to governance he feels best about, and trusting the party leadership and process on this occasion to have made a preliminary and more informed decision for him. But even that requires some degree of very basic knowledge acquired and processed ahead of time.

The fallback strategy of straight party voting in the absence of detailed knowledge about the candidates in a particular election, when possible, would be better than not voting at all, but admittedly not always by much. The obvious disadvantages of relying on that simple approach as a crutch for ignorance cry out for a strategy of problem avoidance instead. Even an hour or two carefully spent on legitimately informational internet sites or a few simple phone calls in advance to a smart, trusted friend can provide lots of answers for the otherwise clueless voter. We should anticipate any upcoming election and get as informed about the issues and candidates as we can. It's not that hard.

&

The ignorance of one voter in a democracy impairs the security of all.
John F. Kennedy

&

When we do go to our local polling place and vote, or fill out an absentee ballot in advance, we should not do so with any misunderstanding, confusion, or lack of awareness over what a vote in a democratic political election really means. Unfortunately, this may be a challenge for some people in our time, and for a surprising reason. One of the biggest hit television shows of the recent past, along with its imitators and spin offs, may unintentionally have redefined and subtly distorted for many of its viewers what exactly a vote is, and what it should mean. I call this, "The American Idol Effect."

For several of its seasons, I loved the show *American Idol*. It was great fun. And I've voted for the contestants on it many times. So have lots of people. I gave Carrie Underwood hundreds of votes at every opportunity. Sorry, Bo Bice. You're great too, I'm sure. I nearly wore out my speed-dial function that season. And in the process of millions of Americans voting for their hopeful American Idol week after week, season after season, in response to the engaging drama of the show, I think many people began to gravitate, whether consciously or not, toward a general misunderstanding of voting that's always a danger in political elections, but that's never been more of a temptation than it was on *American Idol*. And I don't have in mind the assumption that you both can and should vote as many times as possible.

The problem is this: People vote for people they like. Week after week of the vocal competition, viewers send in their votes and many seem to think of each vote as just an expression of personal preference, or even affection. Or, connected with this, they vote to try to help advance the career of the person they find most attractive or likeable, for whatever reason. *American Idol* voters have often reported casting their vote to show how much they enjoy someone's personality, outfits, hair, dance moves, or even quirkiness. "She has such charisma!" Or: "He's so cute!" In response, the famously harsh and perpetually outspoken judge Simon Cowell always insisted to viewers, "This is a *singing* competition, people!" There are qualities we may like in the contestants that simply have nothing to do with the caliber of their vocal performances and talent.

Likewise, in our political elections, there are qualities we may like in candidates that have nothing to do with the purpose of an election. The person you'd most like to have a beer with may be predictably awful as a decision maker in office. There have been times in political campaigns and elections recently when I've wanted to echo Simon and say, "This is a *governance* decision, people!" Some qualities that attract us to candidates bear directly on their capacity to govern well, and others just have nothing to do with it. Intellect is important. General knowledge matters. Character is crucial. Discernment is priceless. A positive vision for the future is indispensable. Kindness counts. Both seriousness and a sense of humor can be relevant. The ability to focus and remain consistent when that's needed, and to adapt when change is better will make a difference. Some measure of wisdom is always a plus. A serious political vote is not meant to be merely an expression of personal preference or affection, or even a way of helping someone we like so that he or she can advance in the world. It's supposed to be about real governance: Who seems best equipped and positioned to represent us well in the complex and demanding business of real governance? Who can most likely get needed things accomplished? A vote is an attempt to make this judgment and selection. It's important to the integrity of the overall process that we vote faithfully and that we vote well, basing our choices on the right considerations.

ღ

Always vote for principle, though you may vote alone, and you may cherish the sweetest reflection that your vote is never lost.
John Quincy Adams

ღ

In our time, we don't have to go deep into researching policy positions to judge the character of a person running for office. Watch the candidates for a few minutes on TV or in a video online. Really listen to what they say and how they say it. Raging insults are a bad sign. Demeaning comments reveal a lot. From the local school board and town council to the state house and halls of Congress, we don't need cages full of preening peacocks and prattling parrots, braying bulls and trash talking toucans. We have to elect compassionate and courageous people of character, whose knowledge runs deep and who can get things done wisely with deliberation and judgment. When choosing sides for a pickup game of hoops, you don't look for loudmouths who can throw insulting labels around, but for those who know what it really takes for excellence, and can pass and rebound and put the ball in the basket. Governance is not about playing to the crowd for laughs, cheers, or boos aimed at opponents. It's about actually getting good things done.

I'm convinced that all the excuses we offer for not participating more in the democratic process, for not giving more thought to our votes, for not doing more in our communities, and for not caring much about anything beyond the ends of our own noses are really just smokescreens around a basic lack of motivation. We have no vision for our nation or strong sense of ourselves as active partners in it. As a result, we lack a sufficiently enthusiastic commitment to safeguarding the things that make possible the freedom we enjoy. And that's a problem well worth solving.

The Declaration of Our Independence

MANY PEOPLE SEEM TO THINK THAT CITIZENSHIP IS JUST A fact and patriotism is no more than a feeling, as if your citizenship is merely a legal fact about where you were born or else sought and attained the requisite status, and patriotism is a separate issue about your customary emotions, or feelings of loyalty and pride. But this is importantly wrong. Citizenship is about a lot more than that. And so is patriotism.

Citizenship is really all about responsibility and privilege. It's a moral matter, not just a legal or political fact, and as such, it's supposed to be a source of ongoing personal involvement and action. Patriotism is a deeply related matter of belief, feeling, attitude, and motivated commitment, all coming together in support of the nation in which you're a citizen, and ultimately in contribution to the larger world in which you live. When our understanding of this is lacking, our motivation is low, our patriotism languishes, and our basic citizenship suffers along with it. Without the proper motivational support, none of us will tend to do what we can, and what we should, for the greater good.

ை

When you cease to make a contribution, you begin to die.
Eleanor Roosevelt

ை

A few years ago, I read something very carefully and thoroughly that, as a result of my newly focused attention, quickly made a big difference in my life. It renewed my sense of what citizenship is and revived my inner patriot. It's actually a document that has made a very big difference for us all, whether we're aware of its details or not. It's our national birth certificate, better known as the Declaration of Independence. One of the greatest political documents in history, this relatively short proclamation launched our nation into its proper place in the world over two hundred years ago. Reading it as an adult, really reading it well and thinking hard about all it says, reignited my sense of what this country stands for and what all of us should care about. It re-established my understanding of what authentic patriotism is and renewed my personal vision for what we can do right now to join the ranks of great Americans through the years.

You may remember first seeing and reading the Declaration of Independence in school a long time ago. But you might not have consulted it again since. It's not the sort of thing most of us consider on any regular basis. And that's a shame, because it contains some extraordinary ideas that relate to our daily lives. Let's look for a moment at the opening statement of that great document, written at a defining moment in our history.

> When in the course of human events it becomes necessary for one people to dissolve the political bands which have connected them with another, and to assume among the powers of the earth the separate and equal station to

which the laws of nature and of nature's God entitle them, a decent respect to the opinions of mankind requires that they should declare the causes which impel them to the separation.

Our predecessors on the scene in the summer of 1776 decided it was time to declare our independence as a nation, to separate ourselves formally from England, and to take our rightful standing in the world as a unified people. Notice from the outset that these founders of our nation understood our status as being one of "equal station," meaning equal rank, status, or position with other nations. They also believed it would be appropriate, out of respect, to explain to the rest of the world what they were doing and why. To accomplish that task, they created and approved this great document, a profound statement of purpose that should continue to be a guiding light for every American in each generation. I was fifty years old before I rediscovered it in a new way and realized its ongoing importance for my life, as well as for the rest of us.

❧

If the American Revolution had produced nothing but the
Declaration of Independence, it would have been worth while.
Samuel Eliot Morrison

❧

On that auspicious day of July 4, 1776, when the final draft of this document was read and approved by our representatives in the Second Continental Congress meeting in Philadelphia, two hundred large-format broadsides of the Declaration were quickly printed in the city to be carried throughout the thirteen original colonies so they could be read and viewed in public places. To my knowledge, only twenty-five of these two hundred originals still exist. Twenty-four are protected in museums or otherwise locked away for their safety and preservation, but the twenty-fifth was discovered just a few years ago, tucked behind a framed picture bought for four dollars at a yard sale, and then sold at auction where it was purchased for eight million dollars by the prominent, ground-breaking creative television producer Norman Lear, who is known widely for his classic American sitcom, *All in the Family,* as well as many other television shows and films. Lear acquired it for the purpose of sending it on a road trip around the country. His idea was that most of us, all in the family of America, might not have easy access to a major museum or library where one of the other originals is on display. Taking this copy around the nation would allow many more people to have the opportunity to see and read in person one of these historic proclamations of our national birth. It was Lear's purchase of the document and his decision to send it around the country that led me to read it anew. He actually called one day and asked if I, as a philosopher, would consider traveling our land with the document and compose a rousing speech about its importance that I could give at every stop it made. I agreed with enthusiasm. But as Norman's team developed the idea of the tour in greater detail and word of it started to spread, some of the most popular actors in Hollywood began to volunteer their services, voices, and celebrity to the tour to attract much more attention to it than a mere philosopher could create. So in the end, I got to stay at home and enjoy it all at a distance. I also had a chance to immerse myself in this amazing document and think through its importance for our day.

When I began to read the Declaration on that occasion for the first time as an adult, it didn't take me long to get excited about what I was seeing in its carefully formulated words. It was bold and forceful in its statements. In fact, the content of the second sentence grabbed me right away:

We hold these truths to be self evident, that all men are created equal, that they are endowed by their creator with certain unalienable rights, that among these are life, liberty and the pursuit of happiness.

With these words, the greatest modern experiment in democracy was launched. With such simple, powerful claims, and those that followed, our founders announced that a new nation is on the map, a country whose whole point of existence is to acknowledge the value and fundamental rights of every human being, and to offer all of us the chance to create our own futures. It proclaimed a nation that from its founding is committed to the ideal of giving each of its citizens the opportunity to live, grow, prosper, and be happy, with the chance to create loving families, great neighborhoods, and good work. This declaration isn't just about the formation of yet another nation among many others existing around the world. It's quite distinctive. It's about a dream. Its ideas are rooted in the best political thought of the ages. And it's about us. It comes to us as a powerful invitation to make a positive difference with our lives, whoever we are, and however we came to be participants in this great endeavor.

∾

America means opportunity, freedom, power.
Ralph Waldo Emerson

∾

Think for a moment about the claim that all men are created equal. We're certainly not all born equal in size, social status, wealth, or talent. We can't sing equally well or speak with the same proficiency, throw a ball with equal accuracy or power, dance with equal grace, or swing a golf club with the same effect. We clearly differ in so many ways. The Declaration of Independence doesn't mean to deny any of this. It just reminds us that we are born with equally great intrinsic value as human beings and, attached to this value, equal basic rights to respect. We are, and should be treated as, equal under the law, with an utterly equal claim of legal protection, born equally worthy of freedom, and equally deserving of the opportunity to grow, prosper, and be happy. We're equally to be considered innocent of any crime until proved guilty, equally deserving of a voice in our communities and country, and equally powerful with that voice when we vote. We equally merit a chance to make a positive difference. And we equally stand to benefit from doing this experiment right.

Thomas Jefferson initially drafted the words that we read in this declaration to express what a great many people in this land had already come to believe by the summer of 1776. We needed a new nation dedicated to these principles. We were ready for a special place on earth to put them into practice, try them out, and then share with the world what we learned as a result. No other nation had been conceived and created for such an explicit reason or with such a determinate vision. We were, from our founding, unique. And because of that, I believe we have a unique role and responsibility in the world, a calling that we can answer and to which we can rise.

༄

The preservation of the sacred fire of liberty, and the destiny
of the republican model of government, is justly considered as deeply,
perhaps as finally, staked on the experiment entrusted
to the hands of the American people.
George Washington

༄

Life, Liberty, and the Great Pursuit

CONSIDER THE PHRASE: "Life, liberty, and the pursuit of happiness." Life is a gift. Liberty is an achievement. The pursuit of happiness, properly understood, is an ongoing process arising from both, and is essential to the highest possibilities that can be found within the human condition.

A gift can be taken away. Any achieved political condition can be lost. A positive process of great importance can be blocked by powerful forces arrayed against it. We've seen vividly in recent years how such forces can imperil liberty and threaten life. For the founders to say that our rights to these conditions are unalienable was to assert that in the deepest nature of things we would always and everywhere have these rights, whether they were recognized and honored by others or not. These remarkable individuals were committed to building a nation and a political structure serving it where such basic human rights would be acknowledged, exercised, and defended. To reaffirm and secure these basic rights anew at our own time in history and to provide for their proper scope in the future, we need to be always vigilant and engaged in their protection in many ways.

The creation of a great nation can never be a one-time event. Of necessity, it is an ongoing process, an extended labor, as successive generations live and refine and apply our founding principles out to the fullest scope of their properly broad reach. In theology, there is a concept of "continuous creation." In politics, we need such an idea as well. The nation building of America is our job now, as it was the job of others in 1776. We now hold the torch and carry the tools. Our founders launched this immense project and bequeathed it to us. It's up to us to defend, develop, and apply our fundamental principles in everything we do. Will the best of who we are elevate the rest of what we do during our time of creative opportunity on earth? It's up to each of us to make this choice.

გ

Americanism consists in utterly believing
in the principles of America.
Woodrow Wilson

გ

We can appreciate the full meaning of the values and principles behind our nation only when we properly understand that the happiness the founders insisted we are free to pursue is not a fragile state of mind or an ephemeral elation of the emotions. It's not simply a feeling of pleasure, a giddy exuberance, or an ease of comfort in the moment. True happiness is much deeper and broader than that. The ancient philosophers who inspired our founders had discovered that real personal happiness is a fundamental state of being. It's the factual, objective reality of a deep overall satisfaction with our life, arising from work that's right for us, supported by relationships that are healthy for us, and augmented by a capacity both to accept each moment for what it is, and then to build something good from where we are at this time. Authentic happiness is a by-product, or a proper side effect, of growth and learning, along with a dose of fun and good work, combined with a resilient ability to embrace good things and people with love and cultivate a capacity to enjoy the process along the way.

This is something that genuinely happy individuals seem to understand. Happiness consists in exercising our talents, flourishing as individuals, and enjoying healthy personal relationships with others. It is a foundation for any form of success worth having. It involves a true prosperity of the spirit, and a goodness of personal intention based on values that matter. In fact, Aristotle once defined happiness as "prosperity combined with virtue." It's the ideal pinnacle of human existence, and according to many great thinkers, a main purpose of our being, as well.

❧

The foolish man seeks happiness in the distance;
the wise man grows it under his feet.
James Oppenheim

❧

Happiness and the American Dream

HAVE YOU EVER WONDERED WHY a foundational political document like the Declaration of Independence would feature so prominently in its opening lines a focus on something like happiness? How did this even get into the mix? What in the world were the founders thinking when they put a mention of something that seems so personal into the opening of a document that's clearly political? Given the full range of concerns they faced, how did something like happiness get such prominent attention as to be named at the outset?

You might even have some misgivings about any connection between happiness and politics at a time now when we face such severe economic, cultural, health, and ecological challenges on the world stage. We're at a point when the most basic right of life itself seems to be under a constant threat from violence of all sorts, from many sources and forces poised against it, and even a minimal experience of true liberty is enjoyed by so few people on earth. It can make us pause to ask whether a pursuit of happiness is even a real possibility for most human beings. And where it is possible, we can be inclined to worry about whether it's perhaps just a bit too self-indulgent a concern or frivolous a focus. That's a thought it's easy to have these days. Pursuing my own happiness in the current state of the world, and everyone else pursuing theirs, can seem so blithely narcissistic. It can appear a little bit like our own personal versions of obliviously dancing in the midst of a storm when more urgent things need attention, or simply doing a modern metaphorical analogue of fiddling while Rome burns.

Aristotle believed that we all naturally seek happiness, or well-being. Many other analysts of the human condition have agreed. It's just a part of who we most deeply are. But in a time of fraught national uncertainty and widespread international anxiety, at a point in history where we face what seem to be uncountable dangers and immeasurable pressures, when nothing is guaranteed and much is needed, it can easily look like happiness is a luxury we can no longer afford. We're struggling to keep our heads above water, our businesses afloat, our families fed and clothed, and our children safe and educated. Then there's old age and a challenge of debility and disease to face, with death an assured outcome of the whole process. Happiness would be nice, but so would a big winning lottery ticket. And many people would find these two things about as likely. But perhaps we should put such worries into a proper perspective.

Let's remember the circumstances under which the Declaration of Independence was written and printed, extolling our right to the pursuit of happiness. The good times did not exactly roll. The basic necessities of life and liberty were by no means firmly in place. It was a time of tremendous uncertainty and constant danger. The authors and approvers of this historic document were spending long periods of time away from the families, friends, and farms they loved, while facing a strong probability of arrest and execution for treason against England as a consequence of their efforts. Their entire enterprise of nation building could collapse and fail, as such endeavors most often do. And, of course, apart from all the many political threats they faced, they lived at a time when various forms of disaster, disease, and death were much more vividly a continued, haunting presence in normal everyday experience than they are for most of us today, even with our modern global health concerns.

These leading citizens of the time knew they would soon enough end their earthly journey, and that the unfriendly companions of pain and suffering would likely be their portal to whatever lay beyond. And yet, they still believed that we all have a fundamental right to the pursuit of happiness, a right so important and relevant to our political life together that it should have a pride of place in the manifesto announcing to the world why we were asserting our national independence and establishing our own domain. They sought a form of life, a broader experience of liberty, and a higher state of being to aspire to as well. For the founders of our nation, happiness was not too much to ask. And in fact, they embraced life and liberty, in part, for the precise purpose of its pursuit.

Similar things could be said of their intellectual progenitor, Aristotle. He didn't live in a bubble of easy bliss. When he detailed the importance of happiness for us all, he knew what this world is like. He understood the difficulties of life. And he built his entire philosophy of human nature around what he saw as our deep and constant quest to be happy. In his estimation, this wasn't just a fleeting feeling, but an ongoing personal state of flourishing, or what we'd now call a deep wellbeing. For the philosopher, happiness was not too much to ask, and failing to pursue it properly was to fail to be fully human.

რ

Happiness is the only sanction of life; where happiness fails,
existence remains a mad and lamentable experiment.
George Santayana

რ

The founders go on to indicate in their declaration that we should think of governments as instituted precisely for the purpose of protecting such personal rights as they enumerate. These rights, including our fundamental right to pursue happiness throughout our days, are that important. The personal and the political are intimately and inextricably interconnected. In fact, to Aristotle, politics is basically about how best we can live well together, with personal fulfillment and community excellence.

Several years ago, I was having breakfast with a group of top American business executives in a private dining area of a great hotel overlooking the Statue of Liberty. That symbol of our nation was outside the window, shining in the early sun. A discussion of national politics arose, and at a certain point I said, "You know, in his great book *The Politics*, Aristotle expressed his view that politics is supposed to be a noble human endeavor focused on how best to live well together." Almost everyone at the table nearly choked on their eggs and toast, or coffee or tea, either gasping or laughing in sudden astonishment. One man replied, "How did we fall so far?" And a deep discussion ensued.

So we have these great words and their associated ideals in our national birth announcement, giving both guidance and guardrails to our choices and actions: "life, liberty, and the pursuit of happiness." It's no accident that this memorable phrase still reverberates through our national life. It has served for over two centuries now to hint at a dream, an aspiration, and a conception of the good for humanity. It hints at a hope for the world arising in a new way within our shores and then spilling beyond, a commitment to create and preserve conditions of common existence that will allow all of us to accept certain minimal and reasonable limits on our behavior in order to live, be free, and pursue our own individual happiness as well as the social conditions that will contribute to the happiness of our families, neighbors, and fellow citizens.

For most of our history here, the American dream has been a vision of personal achievement and enjoyment within the context of a loving family, good friends, and a supportive community. It involves the availability of both individual opportunity and some level of material convenience and comfort for as many as possible. For at least the past century, it has been part of our culture for young people to have dreams of doing something that would make a real difference in their time and, as a result, produce a satisfying degree of prosperity and positive recognition. No other nation has had anything like our self-help, personal growth, or self-improvement literature play such a prominent role in its social life. Regardless of whether you start out from a background of poverty or wealth, the ongoing hope in America has been that you could somehow build your own personal dream life with a measure of security and goodwill supporting it. There have been serious obstacles in the way of that hope for many. But part of the dream is that we can eliminate these impediments as we come to more deeply understand them, and provide the possibility for some version of this dream for all. Living the American dream has been about achieving some measure of success in that quest and enjoying its benefits.

❧

It is neither wealth nor splendor, but tranquility
and occupation, which give happiness.
Thomas Jefferson

❧

In more recent years, we seem to have devolved in our thinking to the point where people have been willing to settle for a cheap counterfeit of success in their dreams and lives, as well as a dim echo of the happiness that naturally accompanies the real thing.

Give us the most glittering side effects—the money, luxury, fame, power, or status—and we'll gladly skip the hard work and real contribution that had always been thought of as essential conditions for the sort of success that was meant to be a part of the authentic American dream. Too many of us have been ready to sacrifice family, friends, and the good of our communities on the altar of external symbols for personal ascendance. And the results have not been good.

What originally was the American Dream? In the age of the founders, it tended to begin with a few acres and a plow—the basic building blocks for an available form of sensible self-reliance that could then play its proper role in a rich, full, and broad community life with family, friends, and neighbors. The dream centered on a vision of decent, fundamentally considerate people pursuing happiness in their own ways and yet helping each other and flourishing together, spiritually as well as physically.

Now, the dream seems to have changed in a most ironic way. Having successfully shed the long historic burden of royalty and designed a superior system of representation, leadership, and service devoid of kings and queens, we then strangely dream to live like monarchs ourselves. We have come to crave the trappings of royalty, the luxuries and fineries of the rich and famous on whatever level we can afford, and even far beyond those bounds. We lust for extravagance, and pursue it heedless of its implications for our environment, our neighbors, our world, and most ironic of all, our own inner selves. We've lost touch with the ancient concept of *enough*. Forgetting the virtue and laudable habit of simplicity has led to a fervent quest for more, with no clear tie to the common good, or even our personal good. This new counterfeit dream has oddly mutated that much from the original, and has had a wide variety of destructive results along the many social, psychological, economic, environmental, and political dimensions of our lives.

Anyone who carefully ponders our culture right now can conclude from personal observation and all available media that this is exactly where we are. For many decades now, we've lived in a land of wildly material dreams. And in this way, we've become a beacon to the world for aspirations of excess. We now have imitators in many nations who keep busy outdoing each other to surpass our own pinnacles of indulgence. We need to get back on a proper course and set a different example for those who notice our ways.

∾

Whatever America hopes to bring to pass in the world
must first come to pass in the heart of America.
Dwight D. Eisenhower

∾

The original American Dream was never at its essence one of mere acquisition, upward mobility, individual success, and social prominence. It was a dream centered on freedom, properly understood, in the forms of both a freedom *from* and a freedom *for*, or expressed slightly differently, a freedom *to*. It focused first on a freedom *from* political tyranny and arbitrary repression, a personal and social liberty that would allow living beyond the unnecessary restrictions of our authoritarian past, and outside any artificial dictates as to what we can be and do. Then second, it envisioned a freedom *for* responsible personal choice, a freedom to live as we choose and seek to create our own version of a good life together, a genuine liberty to pursue adventures in real happiness, with our most prudent decisions and valuable commitments.

After two and a half centuries of struggle and creative political work, we may have seemed to have the first of these freedoms fairly well in hand, at least for the most part, experiencing a freedom from authoritarian tyranny. But in our moment now, it's beginning to become clear that this is certainly a basic liberty that we continually and zealously need to guard. It's never gained once and for all. And yet, the second freedom is arguably our primary challenge now, a freedom for happiness, a liberty to actually flourish and be well. And its realization, after all, is the central purpose of the first freedom. We escaped oppression in order to live fully our best potential.

I think it's important to understand the deep connection between these two forms or aspects of freedom. Let's call "freedom from" by the name of 'permissive freedom,' since it permits the free choice of our own paths in the world, and let's refer to "freedom for or to" with the phrase 'purposive freedom.' Permissive freedom allows us the room to chart our own directions forward through a combination of spontaneity, deliberation, and choice, while purposive freedom inspires and guides that spontaneity, deliberation, and choice with a measure of vision, conviction, and hope. It's obvious how the former allows for the latter. But the latter also protects the former. Without a purposive vision, permissive freedom can perish. A sense of higher purpose sustains liberty. When it's absent, various forces can chip away at our basic freedom and erode the conditions in which alone it can flourish and supply the full framework within which the pursuit of happiness is possible.

It is this higher form of purposive freedom, a freedom to pursue happiness and live a good life, that is actually the essential core of the real American Dream, and the best social and political aspiration of people in every part of the world. It's a dream of positive possibilities and of proper human growth and self-actualization together, consisting in the cultivation of both strong individuals and vibrant communities. It's a vision of open opportunities for our children and their children into the future. It is the ideal of a form of life where some degree of material safety and basic prosperity is a resource for human flourishing and spiritual health, and where our immense creativity aims at social as well as personal enrichment. It's about doing something meaningful and having some real satisfaction in the process.

☙

Human felicity is produced not so much by great pieces of good fortune that seldom happen, as by little advantages that occur every day.
Benjamin Franklin

☙

The American Dream is all about the broadest chance for our mutual fulfillment in the deepest possible sense. And it's really about what it means to live a good life together. Unless we understand that, we'll be hard pressed to make the right political and personal decisions in the future. With a vivid renewal of this vision for ourselves and our freedom, we can revitalize our sense of citizenship and patriotism for our time. Without it, we're vulnerable to a nightmarish alternative where freedom is misunderstood as a libertine anarchy to be secured by forms of threat and intimidation that break up communities and block any possibility of a widespread common good. And that, to put it mildly, was not the vision of our founders, or of anyone with a sound mind.

In my work as a public philosopher over the past decades, I've come to realize that true success in any individual's life and work is never just a personal and individual accomplishment, and neither is real happiness. The highest and deepest forms of success and happiness are always made possible both by our individual freedom and by the opportunities that our social and political context provides for us to grow strong and work well with others, using our hearts and minds and hands to do real good in the world. Our outer circumstances set the stage for our best adventures, and offer us the resources we can use to attain the higher goals that matter to us most.

That's the way it is in life. Where you live can determine what you can do and who you can become. Your social and political context can allow your dreams to come true, or keep you from even having a chance. The best surroundings can magnify your shot at success in anything you do. And that is precisely what our great country was designed to provide for as many of us as possible. Despite our many flaws and deep imperfections, we've gotten so many of the basic ideals right. They are the fundamental values that are expressed in our Declaration of Independence and should be embodied in our attitudes, actions, and votes. We can make this country and our lives increasingly better if we determine to live these values each day. It's our responsibility to do so.

☙

The time for action is now. It's never too late
to do something.
Antoine de Saint-Exupery

☙

Real American Patriotism

A LITTLE CHILD IN OUR LAND can grow up to be a recognized hero—a healer, a teacher, an inventor, a great athlete, a visionary business founder, a powerful leader, a creative role model—or simply a good person and strong citizen: a great friend, wonderful parent, reliable worker, and kind neighbor. Any young person can do something to make the world better. Even if we start in small ways, we can end up making a big difference. Everything is possible for us here. We can dream and do and succeed in a remarkable way, thanks to the freedoms we enjoy. Real American patriotism understands this. It works to secure, enhance, and embody the values that make this liberty and life possible.

Patriotism is most basically defined as, simply, "a love of your country." But we need to be clear about what this means. Genuine patriotism isn't just a loyal state of mind or a warm inner feeling. It's not merely an attitude of approval and support. And it's never simply one more form of clannish pride or enthusiastic fandom. It's an inner determination and commitment to act for the good of our country, together with an outer pattern of ongoing action that delivers real value into the world. It's a beneficial involvement in the dynamic life of our nation and beyond, on however small or large a scale. It's supportive and creative. And it isn't meant to be exclusionary. I love my children, but that of course doesn't mean I can't also love other children as well. This is, in fact, a vitally important point to make in our day. The real American patriot pays attention to the needs of his neighbors and listens as well to the concerns of the world. He or she then takes action to do something positive about problems that cry out for solution, whether on the local scene, in our national life, or elsewhere on the much broader world stage. Patriotism, as a form of love, embraces what's nearby and cares about what's far away, as mutually relevant to the good of all.

ᘓ

I venture to suggest that patriotism is not a short and frenzied
outburst of emotion but the tranquil and steady
dedication of a lifetime.
Adlai E. Stevenson

ᘓ

This point is worth elaborating. A full-bodied sense of patriotic affiliation, combined with a strongly noble attitude of loyalty, doesn't have to involve any divisive or antagonistic exclusivity of concern whatsoever. It's not meant to be a new form of tribalism on just a bigger scale. It's a matter of tending our garden wherever we live, and offering its beauty and bounty to all. It's about working on our small piece of the world, our little spot in the cosmos, and offering it up to the larger context as our own little bit of art, our gift to the bigger picture within which we all live and work.

I like to think of our proper moral spheres of concern and care as represented by concentric circles, each inner one supporting and contributing to the next and larger one out beyond its borders. Proper patriotism operates at many levels, from the individual to the international, and at several stages in between. At the innermost circle, particular individuals who are stronger, healthier, more balanced, ethically and spiritually developed, wise, loving, and loyal make for stronger and better families and friendships. Better families and networks of friends then can create together stronger neighborhoods and communities; better communities make for a better and stronger nation; and properly stronger nations can join together positively and powerfully to create a better world. Each level supports the next one out, and each larger circle of concern should then reach back and care for the integrity and health of any inner circles supporting it. A flourishing at every level can then be possible. This picture of inner and outer circles can be used productively to understand life in general, and also life inside any organization, such as a business or governmental agency. Health requires contribution and care across circles.

ℭℌ

To put the world right in order, we must first put the nation in order;
to put the nation in order, we must first put the family in order;
to put the family in order, we must first cultivate our personal life;
we must first set our hearts right.
Confucius

ℭℌ

This is what I like to call "The Inner Circle Principle." Building good relations in our innermost circles of family, friends, neighbors, and co-workers can form the basis for creating better relations on a broader scale as well, moving outward from where we start. A broadest possible concern for the entire world does not require any lack of concern for home, or a less than enthusiastic embracing of our own heritage and land. In addition, a sense of robust appreciation and goodwill for our homeland never has to end at its borders. A Frenchman can love France without denigrating everyone else. A Russian can embrace his ancient heritage and deeply love his native land without at all adopting any sort of adversarial posture toward other nations and lands. Love seeks to include. An American can love our country both for its own sake and for the sake of the world.

Racism, sexism, regionalism, religious sectarianism, and divisive politics are all forms of a dangerous tribalism that involves being stuck in a narrow circle and sapping its own health. The best patriotism, like a proper loyalty to any of our affinity groups, is outwardly open and expansively contributive. It's all about making a positive difference to something greater than the self, and to something broader than the smallest circle of society within which we happen to live. This kind of patriotism seeks to contribute to the greater good of others both within and beyond the local and national boundaries of its first concerns and commitments. It always looks toward a broader good. The patriotism we can believe in and commit to is inherently invitational. It isn't narrowly prejudiced, stubbornly arrogant, or militantly aggressive. It's never a simple binary, dichotomized, adversarial view of "us against them." It's not the same thing as a narrow and dangerous nationalism. It isn't a fortress mentality. It's not essentially confrontational or accusatory. It isn't based on worry, fear, distrust, or hate. Instead, patriotism of the best sort is rooted in the deepest values that ultimately can unite rather than divide. And that's of course what love is. It's a readiness to put our best values into action and celebrate their importance for a life of significance. Since politics can stir passion and tempt our lower emotions to take control, it's important that any worthy call to patriotic engagement be understood as an invitation to cultivate our best instincts rather than to indulge our worst.

Patriotism is really a form of productive partnership, as Aristotle helps us to grasp. In fact, you can read his book *The Politics* as elaborating this in various ways. A simple formula can be extracted from his profound musings that presents the highest of worldly accomplishment as always coming from, in my own simple words, a dynamic threefold structure of:

People in Partnership for a Shared Purpose.

THE PINNACLE OF HUMAN GREATNESS is never just the result of a sole individual in solitary work, but always comes from a plurality of involved people. And those people have to be in a certain relation to each other, that of real partnership or collaboration, working together. Finally, a partnership is best founded and guided by a shared vision or purpose for which the partners work. That's patriotism at its essence. It's a cooperative endeavor, and not the relentless competition or even combat that our current "culture wars" can make it seem. Not everything is a zero-sum game to be won or lost. The gamification of modern politics has not been a healthy development. But we too often treat elections as about our team winning and the other team losing, whatever it might take to get that result. People cheer at political rallies the way they do at football or basketball games. But such entertainment isn't the form of engagement that a responsible participation in mature governance requires. Politics wasn't meant to be a cutthroat bloodspot. George Washington was worried that having political parties would result in exactly that sort of thing and lead to an artificial affiliation or misguided loyalty that can disconnect us altogether from the greater good of our nation.

You may have read the ancient Greek classic poem, *The Iliad*, when you were in high school or college, or maybe as an adult later in life. It's about the mythical Trojan War, and many readers are stunned at the vivid violence relentlessly depicted in its lines. But it's not just about guts and glory, or the constantly shifting fortunes of opponents as they alternately win or lose battles along the way, soon to have their fate reversed again, and then again. It's really about the power of partnership. And it conveys this theme in a number of powerful ways.

The story opens when the fighting has been going on for many years and the original sense of partnership among the Greek leaders besieging Troy has begun to fray. In fact, the two most powerful figures in the story, the chief military leader Agamemnon and the top warrior Achilles, have become resentful and angry toward each other, even furious. Their own selfish concerns have shattered their crucial collaboration, and terrible harm for many is the result. By contrast, there are small episodes all through the epic story where a powerful warrior is attacked by a group of enemies and he calls on his comrades to join him in the fight, who then all partner up together to succeed.

ↄ

Alone we can do so little; together we can do so much.
Helen Keller

ↄ

The Iliad has been called the greatest anti-war story ever written, and precisely because it so graphically depicts the tragic and immensely violent waste of lives that are merely cut down on the field of battle and prematurely taken out of the world that their talents and minds could have improved for years or decades into the future. The poem displays the destructiveness of a violent, adversarial mentality in many ways, and yet in one small passage, it also hints at a solution and way out.

In an often overlooked scene, two men confront each other on the field of battle, but before either can attack, one calls out that he has watched his adversary earlier and is so impressed with his prowess that he must know the man's name and history. The fighter he addresses is confused and hesitant to comply. But in a very short time, he agrees and begins to tell his story with an account of where he's from, and describes his father and grand-father. The other soldier says, basically, "Wait. My grandfather knew your grandfather. They were friends. Yours did mine a great favor. We're connected. We can't fight each other." The other man agrees. They even pledge mutual protection and trade armor as a sign of their respect for each other and their new commitment. They ceased to be adversaries when each became fully human to the other. They no longer thought of the other as "enemy," but as a real person, an equal with a good history and values and even ties that linked them together beyond the purposes of the battle being fought around them. We need to remember this story in our day. Most political differences shouldn't be thought of in starkly adver-sarial ways. People who vote differently are not thereby enemies to be slandered and fought. We're all human beings with stories and ties that can unite us in many ways, once we see through the cate-gories and concerns that divide us. We do well to resist any insults and names that diminish, disrespect, or dehumanize those who are politically different from us. We should seek to know their stories, and try to understand what connects us beneath our differences.

Real patriots don't fight each other any more than good gar-deners do. They find what they have in common and build on it. They try to understand each other and seek ground on which they all can stand and work. They make an effort to arrive at some mutual understandings based on higher values, and may even learn that they can engage in common projects beyond the areas of their disagreement. And in the end, as we realize and remember this, we will understand that we all need to work to preserve a culture and political process where we can indeed freely disagree, discuss, and even debate, without undue ego or enmity, and avoid allowing our varying opinions to degenerate into the adversarial mindset whose destructive consequences were so clearly on display long ago on the bloody plain outside the walls of the mythical and instructive Troy.

Our Fundamental Values

WHAT ARE THE VALUES OF A REAL AMERICAN PATRIOT? There are many, but I believe that seven stand at the core of our distinctive national vision: Life, Liberty, Equality, Opportunity, Justice, Security, and Service. A brief look at each of these values will fill out our understanding of what a genuinely beneficial form of patriotism seeks to represent and secure for the greater good.

The Value of Life

Americans celebrate life. At our best, we value and protect it wherever we can. We seek to enrich and preserve it, and help make it worth living. At least, we do this when we are consistently acting in harmony with the core of our founding vision. This is why we have been among the first through modern history to rush to the aid of any nation or group whose lives have been threatened or shattered by war, natural calamity, or disease. In a deep, general, and abiding sense, America has always been profoundly "pro-life," whenever it has been true to its fundamental values. And I don't use this phrase to mean anything political or controversial, but something universal.

༄

*The care of human life and happiness, and not their destruction,
is the first and only legitimate object of government.*
Thomas Jefferson

༄

Our ongoing differences over the moral status of various controversial medical procedures and related issues involving death, especially forms of care that raise questions about when distinctively personal human life begins and how it properly can end, should never be allowed to obscure the basic fact that we all care about life. There are deep issues concerning the existence and nature of a soul, or what makes for a fully human life, that turn on philosophical questions that can never be solved by anything like a proof that will convince all sincere and reasonable people of one and only one true answer. From the prenatal state to questions over the alleviation of suffering in the terminally ill, genuinely good people hold divergent views over what is permissible or obligatory. We live in a world of uncertainty, and that may be not a flaw, but a feature of our existence. It's only amid many uncertainties that we are provoked to dig deep and cultivate some of our most important inner attitudes, emotions, and virtues like courage, empathy, and faith. We should resist the cheap, false certainties that many offer us these days, pandering to our fears and assuming we can't face the reality of not always having answers in an absolute sense. On each side of every divisive issue regarding the sanctity of life, there are those who want to protect or enhance it in some way. That's just the ultimate baseline culture of who we as Americans and as human beings are.

Some of our moral concerns legitimately become the basis of law. Where there is broad and general moral agreement, legislation can often be both important and practical. But other moral concerns that may rightly feel just as vital and urgent can be lived and shared and promoted without our insisting that they be captured in legislation, if there isn't enough widespread agreement among sincere, morally sensitive, and well-informed people in order to make that a reasonable goal. And most such issues are badly handled if we allow them to prevent all the other cooperation and partnership that a harmonious community life, or having a great nation, requires. Some matters are deeply personal, though perhaps also of public interest or concern. And not everything that's a moral issue needs to be a matter of legal coercion, a policy and process that rarely works, in the end, with anything whose ultimate status is widely disputed in the populace. While we can all understand the one issue voter who cares deeply about a single matter viewed as of supreme importance, we also have to recognize how the unscrupulous among us can pander to such voters in ways that disguise their true motives and agendas. When we operate from an assumption that most people have legitimate interests and good values underlying their personal concerns, we can learn to cooperate on the things we have in common without allowing our differences to pull apart the hope of a healthy and harmonious common life.

೮ා

Controversial disputes are a part of democratic culture.
Angela Merkel

೮ා

We want to provide a place where life can be rich and rewarding for ourselves and our families, as well as for our fellow citizens and visitors. We value anything that will allow and encourage a form of life full of positive possibilities and supportive of the happiness that is our proper quest. And we want to promote such conditions around the world whenever we can do so in a way that's compatible with all our foundational values and also sensitive to other cultures, while respecting the deepest needs of human nature. We believe that life is to be treasured and enhanced as much as possible, so that a fullness of potential is available for all.

The Value of Liberty

In the eyes of the world, America also at its best stands for liberty, the freedom of all people to respond to life with the best that's within them, the social space to discover their talents, develop those talents, and deploy them into the world for the good of others as well as themselves. This concern for liberty in the explicitly stated ideals of our nation involves a freedom to learn and grow and flourish, as well as to be involved in creating together the structures and rules under which we all can live well. We believe that individuals should be as free as possible to choose their own way in the world, in so far as that is compatible with an equal freedom for others. It's all about selecting our proper paths, without having them dictated to us by the authority and force of others. In a deep, general, and abiding sense, America has always been supportive of both choice and life.

We too often seem to view and exercise our liberty as if it were no more than a lack of constraints. The core of proper political freedom is not a chaos of limitless indulgence. And most of us know that, but we need to live more consistently with what we understand. Freedom and order are not opposites, but are to be understood in ways that are mutually supportive. Any freedom that's of value will respect and safeguard the sort of order required to make it possible to have, live, and use well. Any order that's healthy for a society or a life will encourage and allow for proper forms of freedom. As positive and healthy states of human existence, freedom and order each require and inwardly strengthen each other. They are deeply entwined and engaged.

႟

Freedom makes a huge requirement of every human being.
With freedom comes responsibility.
Eleanor Roosevelt

႟

Liberty isn't just about an absence of something bad, but also the potential for something good. It faces in two directions at once, covering dual polarities of concern. Freedom from authoritarian oppression, unjust force, and undue restraint is meant to provide for a wide range of positive values and purposes that can be acknowledged by the free individual. Then, the nobility of purpose we choose to embrace is what gives our freedom its high worth. The possibilities and opportunities provided by our fundamental political liberty must be used properly, which means responsibly and well. And it is only liberty that's lived appropriately that will both contribute to our own overall wellbeing and attract, inspire, and sustain the regard of the wider world.

The responsibilities, requirements, or duties implicitly inherent in freedom are all about creating and maintaining the conditions in which freedom can continue to flourish for others as well as ourselves. The free person is called to play a small part in making freedom available as widely as possible. Liberty is both release and responsibility.

႟

Freedom has its life in the heart, the actions, the spirit of men,
and so it must be daily earned and refreshed—else like a flower
cut from its life giving roots, it will wither and die.
Dwight D. Eisenhower

႟

The Value of Equality

America as a created, constructed democratic enterprise also aims at the fundamental value of equality. Our nation was founded ideally and practically to recognize, respect, and defend the basic equality of all human beings that's to be found beneath or behind our great and numerous differences and inequalities. This is a value we've failed to live well for a very long time around such matters as race, religion, gender, and personal ability, and we've come to approximate it slightly better only with the many generations since our founding. It's a value dear to the younger people in our population who are especially keen on expanding its reality in the world. It's also a proper universal commitment, a natural source of worldly hope, and a great strength for our future. The fact that we still struggle to respect this value more than two centuries after our founding should be no surprise, given the sad realities of human history that arise out of both individual and social psychology. But this disappointing truth should be no cause for a cynical doubt about the ultimate realism of having equality as a guiding ideal.

☙

Four score and seven years ago, our fathers bought forth
on this continent a new nation, conceived in liberty,
and dedicated to the proposition that all men are created equal.
Abraham Lincoln

☙

At many times in our ancient past, our distant ancestors lived in circumstances of threat and looming scarcity. That naturally bred in them a habit of hoarding resources and opportunities as a matter of life or death. This instinctive possessiveness could be a matter of the individual, the family group, or the tribe. It was easy to then view anyone outside the inner circle as unequal in rights or value relative to scarce and needed goods. Any such concern of self-preservation easily becomes about inequality in some form, where our focus is narrowed, more exclusive, and backed by fear. But moral growth ultimately requires going beyond such a perspective. The contrasting value of equality is all about respect, honor, fairness, availability, and hope extended to all. No community can flourish over time without it as a high ideal and guiding value.

The increasing election of African-American, Asian, and Latino citizens to local, state, and national offices can be fully appreciated at this moment in our history only against the backdrop of our long fight to overcome the ugly legacies of slavery and the stubborn prejudices of negative racial attitudes that even now hold us back. It's a real and powerfully symbolic culmination of long and ongoing efforts to firmly establish our founding value of equality as something more than a rhetorical hope and distant dream. Many of us older Americans have lived long enough to see important civil rights legislation introduced, resisted, fought, passed, enforced, and then eroded during our lifetimes. We still need to work hard to achieve this crucial value more consistently and at the highest levels. Implemented better and more normally, the core value of equality can act as a truly remarkable and energizing ideal and reality for us all.

∤

We will never have true civilization until
we have learned to recognize the rights of others.
Will Rogers

∤

The Value of Opportunity

The value of equality is tied up with that of opportunity. Equality has to do with more than fair treatment under the law. In

America, we believe that every human being comes into this world equally deserving of the chance to grow and flourish and make a positive difference. Because of that, we should seek to provide everyone with the fundamentals of real opportunity for personal development, individual contribution, and appropriate success. This founding intention is why we have long been known around the world as "The Land of Opportunity," and are still so viewed by many. Our basic economic system, our social structures, and our attitudes should allow for forms of access to personal growth and achievement that are still not available in many places across the globe.

Cynics can easily point out that any concept of "equal opportunity for all" is in the strictest sense a mirage and a practical impossibility. Some of us are born to wealth; others arrive in poverty. Our places of origin, and the networks of relationships into which we are born and grow can make a lot of difference in terms of the opportunities we have along the way. The particular people in our lives present us with different chances. The world is too complex and our differences are too many and varied in order for all inequalities of opportunity to be eliminated and a uniformity of open doors to be provided for all. Many opportunities are a matter of serendipity, synchronicity, or fortuitous happenstance. The person you happen to meet on the street, in a shop or café, on social media, or on a plane might change your life in a way that's simply unavailable to anyone who was not in that place at that time, and so missed the exact conversation that led to an amazing chance to develop or to serve the world. But our ideals don't lack value because they're not perfectly realizable in an absolute form. They're just supposed to guide us well. It's their function to spur us on, to give us direction, and to move us positively beyond where we already are. Yes, it's true that we'll never be able to provide exactly equal opportunities for all people. But when building a society that will provide some sort of open and helpful opportunity for everyone is seen as a basic personal, community, and national value, we allow ourselves to grow strong and healthy as a result.

And yet, again, a real opportunity for growth and achievement that's open to all throughout the land is often still more of an aspiration than an actuality in the lives of too many of our citizens. But it is a legitimate dream and a driving hope within our shores. Opportunity is, in its many dimensions, a vital value supporting the American endeavor. The more broadly it's made available to individuals and communities, the better we all can flourish together. I think the philosophy of our founding commits us to its importance as a fundamental value. And it's in everyone's enlightened self-interest to promote the spread of opportunity throughout society. We can all benefit from the good growth and achievements of others. We need to work to make sure that the availability of opportunity does not wane in our time, but that it can increase for the benefit of all.

The Value of Justice

Justice is also a core American value. The main body of the Declaration of Independence details the felt injustices that led us as a people to break our ties to a faraway government ignoring our legitimate concerns, and to constitute ourselves as a sovereign nation in pursuit of the justice we had not otherwise been able to find. A good part of the intent behind our ancestors' push for independence was to establish a government and society in which greater justice overall could prevail.

࿇

Justice is what love looks like in public.
Cornel West

࿇

Here again, this is not something we can claim to have attained in any degree remotely close to what our founders at their best had hoped for, and that we still desire. But it is something to which we as Americans should be committed, and toward which we must strongly work and aspire.

Injustice can cripple a community and blight any nation that tolerates it. It can block the best possibilities of life together. And yet it's a nearly guaranteed natural consequence of extreme wealth and power disparities among people. It's also something that's found in nearly every culture and time, despite the fact that most people seem to come into the world with an innate tendency to reject it, except perhaps when it appears to favor them. And of course, this is the real rub and snare where the tangled skein of human nature trips up progress toward our highest ideals. Too many people prefer to see justice prevail merely outside those cases when its opposite promises to benefit them more. But a deeper understanding of our condition reveals that unjust deeds can never truly benefit their perpetrators or anyone else, something we can grasp only when mere appearances are rolled back and all things are considered. Unjust circumstances never place anyone at a real and lasting advantage, despite any superficial illusions that might exist to the contrary. As Socrates taught us long ago, it's bad to suffer from wrong behavior, but it's much worse to engage in it. No one can flourish as a result of it. Tolerating, creating, or exploiting any lack of justice in human relations simply corrupts the soul, damaging any perpetrator or enabler within his or her own innermost being, and nothing can do greater harm than that. It also diminishes us all in the bargain by weakening the social fabric within which we live and move, and on which we depend.

As American citizens, we're to be on the watch for injustice, and to do whatever we morally can to see basic justice prevail in our everyday conduct, in our business dealings, in our communities, and throughout our larger national life. Is everyone being treated as fairly as possible? Are the circumstances of our life together being monitored in such a way as to respect what justice demands? To embrace justice as a founding American value is to be committed to living it out as a daily concern. In this country, justice is supposed to be everybody's business, guided by the letter and spirit of our most enlightened laws, but going beyond the details of the law whenever needed.

The Value of Security

Security is a basic political value precisely because it is the condition needed in order for life to be sustained, liberty to flourish, equality to be respected, broad opportunity to be provided in a full ongoing way, and justice to prevail. It is only under these conditions that a full and proper pursuit of happiness is possible for each of us, for those we love, and for the overall communities in which alone we can truly flourish.

೮⁄೨

If we are looking for insurance against want and oppression,
we will find it only in our neighbors' prosperity and goodwill and,
beyond that, in the good health of our worldly places, our homelands.
Wendell Berry

೮⁄೨

The security we speak of here is a matter of many things. It obviously involves a sound and forward thinking foreign policy, scientifically well-informed environmental practices and sustainable energy programs, strong homeland preparedness, broad military readiness, a robust network of well functioning intelligence capabilities through which we can discover and assess developing threats, and locally effective, service-oriented police, public safety, and fire departments. It also requires, just as importantly, rational, trustworthy, and effective courts, a robust educational system, reliable energy and weather services, a free press providing us with an abundant flow of needed information, fundamental economic stability, innovative business cultures, and high quality available healthcare. National security ultimately depends on all these things. When the basic security of our citizens and visitors is a real value, we are committed as patriotic Americans to improving and maintaining every one of these diverse but important aspects of our national life. No part of the founding framework ensconced in our national constitution was meant to erode our basic security, but only and always to provide for it.

Considering together a representative array of basic national values allows us to appreciate their many inter-connections and refine our understanding of each. A good measure of security is needed for the sustenance of life as well as for its full enjoyment. Any process, polity, practice, or apparatus aimed at our security that somehow ends up needlessly endangering or diminishing our life together would be inconsistent with that important value for the sake of which it's embraced. Not all systems or situations claimed to enhance our security will actually accomplish that, rather than resulting in the very opposite. We need to be vigilant to assess as well and as carefully as we can what will in fact accomplish the support and preservation of the measure of security we all deserve.

In a parallel way, our concern for national security is meant to protect our liberty, not subvert it. Conversely, our understanding of liberty must be compatible with the need for the security without which it can't exist. Each value must coordinate with the other. An overall dynamic harmony of our national values is possible, and it's also of vital importance. Any one of them must be understood, developed, and implemented in a manner consistent with the others. We can reasonably differ on how this harmony is to be attained, but agreement on everything was never expected of us, only a measure of respectful cooperation in seeking the right forms of balance. The whole cluster of values underlying our founding and honoring its concerns constitutes the basis and guiding framework for the great and original American Dream.

ぐ

The only liberty I mean, is a liberty connected with order;
that not only exists along with order and virtue,
but which cannot exist at all without them.
Edmund Burke

ぐ

The Value of Service

At the heart of a robust everyday patriotism and a rich sense of citizenship is the value of service: service to our family members, friends, neighbors, communities, and nation. This fundamental American value is meant in addition to extend ultimately into a service to the world. We owe other people our lives. Others brought us into this realm of existence, provided us with a rich context in which we could grow, thrive, and be free, and ask nothing more in return than that we keep this in mind as we make our choices day to day.

Human civilization is of course more interconnected now than ever before, and our actions can help or hinder others around the world to a degree not dreamed of in the past. The value of service has no boundaries or borders. It starts near and reaches far. When we simply treat others the way we would want to be treated if we were in their place, we adopt the basic orientation of service that is so crucial for our time.

༄

*The best way to find yourself is to lose yourself
in the service of others.*
Gandhi

༄

We can serve our family members and neighbors in many simple ways. Take out the trash. Recycle. Conserve energy, and not just by putting your feet up in a position of repose. Cut the grass. Wash the dishes. Pick up litter. Do something to help a friend. Volunteer at a school or in a community program. If you have pets, train them well. Care for them and clean up after them. Make sure their actions don't seriously diminish the quality of your neighbors' lives. Speak to everyone with kindness in so far as possible, and keep in mind it almost always is. The good citizen and everyday patriot is concerned about the mundane and the majestic, the everyday and the exalted. Little things add up.

We have been well served in countless respects by individuals who came before us in the course of the human adventure and our national endeavor. It's our duty and great privilege to return the favor and act in service to all now living and still others yet to be born. Our government on every level exists as well for the sole purpose of serving us all, and never just a few. It is for this service that we give it our hearty consent, our best corrective ideas, and our allegiance. After all, in a democracy like ours, government isn't really a separate entity on its own, but is just a structure and set of resources and processes by which we serve each other, and thereby ourselves, on a bigger scale than we otherwise can manage. When we do it right, governments are us.

A Message
to the World

As we've all been vividly reminded in recent years, and in terribly unforgettable ways, there are people in the world who misunderstand or seem to simply hate our values. Some fear our freedoms. Others despise our faults. Many define us in terms of our worst decisions rather than our greatest accomplishments or highest aspirations, and dream of bringing our enterprise to an end. A multitude of them want our ongoing experiment in democracy to fail. And they seek more than anything else to turn us against each other. Some of them have killed thousands of our fellow citizens in various ways and on numerous occasions. More than a few of them would prefer the toll to be millions. They've already left far too many little boys and girls without parents, husbands without wives, moms without dads, and devoted friends with huge gaping holes in their lives. But they haven't left the rest of us without options. I believe we need to send a clear message to all of them, and to any around the world who cheer them on, as well as to the many in our time around our own nation who just sit on the sidelines, uninterested and disengaged. And we need to send this message today, tomorrow, and each day after that.

♥ᴐ

We must meet our duty and convince the world
that we are just friends and brave enemies.
Thomas Jefferson

♥ᴐ

There are some things that have happened in our country in the past few decades that show America at its best. And there have been many other developments that reveal us at our worst. The better things display an affirmation of humanity in all its positive diversity and a new more productive focus for the future. They announce that we value ideas, intellect, creativity, kindness, justice, equality, and that basic respect for other nations that our founders thought to be so important. They communicate a new and growing spirit of positive engagement and collaborative solution directed at our thorniest problems. But we all need to follow this implicit message with a further clear and powerful statement of intent. We need to demonstrate by our actions that we truly believe in the values of our nation and plan to live them well. It's time to signal that we want the best for each other and our country right now, and that we desire it in part because we want the best for the world. Those among us who are greedy for power, fame, and wealth at the expense of everything else would lead us callously and cynically down precisely all the wrong paths. They say the words their followers want to hear, and often pretend to champion values that matter, and so seek to hide the dangerous manipulators they are. But one solid test is this: If they appeal to fear, fan flames of anger, hurl wild accusations, and clearly serve to encourage division and distrust, they are not at all likely working for us and our greater common good, but rather seeking to exploit the rest of us for their badly misguided sense of self-interest. We need to judge better when to turn away.

If we can show our global neighbors what the free citizens and patriots of a real democracy are willing and able to accomplish in support of values that can benefit us all, we can give people in our time a new view of what America is and what we can accomplish together. It can also be a hint as to what any nation can aspire to as well. We need to send out a message that will show our fundamental solidarity with the best supporters of humanity everywhere, and our equal determination to resist all its oppressors. Such a message will tend to elicit the support we need from our neighbors and friends around the world in order to have the best positive impact we can.

We will not be deceived, bullied, or threatened into quitting. We will never be cowed and defeated by the misunderstandings, mistaken hatreds, floods of insidious misinformation, and misplaced violence directed against us and those who share our values. We will continue. We will grow and improve. And by adopting policies and actions true to our highest dreams and deepest values, in partnership with friends of the human spirit around the world, we can prevail.

America certainly isn't even close to being a perfect place. We all know that, and it's why we seek positive change. But in many ways, at its core, in its essential promise and its ongoing struggle to live that promise, it's a distinctively promising place, and we can all take action to make it better. This is a swath of the globe where almost anything is possible. This is a land where initiative, persistence, innovation, and love can conquer hate, overcome misunderstanding, correct mistakes, and build something new, noble, and of great lasting value. And certainly, that's easy to say but hard to do. Ideals are like that.

We need to send a signal to the world and each other with our actions as well as our words. We need to get a message out to our own population and the whole globe that we truly believe in this nation and in all the values for which it stands, that we are committed to its health, and that we intend to stand by its promise, and to stand by each other in our worst difficulties as well as our best times. We do believe in the great enterprise of democracy that our nation represents. And so we should now invite each other, and the rest of the world, to see how we can strive anew to live our values every day. We can't do that by just employing the rhetoric of our ideals. We need to demonstrate to each other and the broader world the real thing now.

We believe in the human spirit. We fundamentally believe in each other. And, ultimately, we are committed to the whole human family. As Americans, it's our calling, our opportunity, and our duty to demonstrate these beliefs in action. That's what the bold enterprise of representative democracy is all about. And that's why there is one thing we should focus on and seek at every opportunity to do very well.

❧

Someone struggled for your right to vote.
Use it.
Susan B. Anthony

❧

So, then, what can we do now? What can we do to show each other and the wider human community the way we really feel about our great national adventure and its proper place in the bigger picture of international affairs? The answer is simple. We can exercise, as comprehensively as possible, the power of our distinctively democratic right to vote, and in new ways that many of us have never considered as such. We can vote in many different forms, and there is an important and perhaps surprising sense in which we can do this every day. At the heart of active citizenship and true patriotism is a habit we need to cultivate, and it's precisely the actions generated by this habit that will send our proper message to each other and then out to the larger world. The real key to patriotism and the foundation of our future is to vote in some real sense every day.

Voting Every Day

VOTE IN THE NEXT ELECTION. Vote in every election. Vote even when there is no election! But of course, in a deeper sense, there is always an election. The words 'elect' and 'election' come from an ancient Latin root (the verb: *elego, elegere*) that meant to choose or pick out. We need to think of our daily actions as the result of what we have chosen to do, what we have picked out of all available alternatives as worth our time and attention. And we should choose things that will be of benefit to our communities and our nation, to each other, and to the world. Elect the right matters of concern. Choose needed actions. Vote with your time, your attention, your conversation, and your energies, day to day. Read the paper, keep up with the more reliable news sources that have been around a long time and are staffed by well-trained journalists, sites that were not created simply for narrowly partisan interests; keep up on the problems and opportunities of the day; and get involved in your community to help with the many solutions to local challenges that are required for a better life together. Notice all the needs and challenges that exist around you. Take action, do something good, and by your deeds as well as your words, you can make your views known. And of course, by doing the same things, so can I.

❧

Action is eloquence.
William Shakespeare

❧

When I get worked up about a national or regional issue and think my voice should be heard, I write my Congressional representative or senator. Maybe you've done this too. And I know it can be frustrating. We get these form letters back ("Dear Constituent") and that can be disheartening. But don't be discouraged. Even if you want to write your elected representatives a form letter yourself, voice your views. I've even sent emails that are as succinct as "Stop lying." Sadly, my advice was not taken. "We appreciate your letter," they lied. But it was worth a try. Communicate your concerns in as many ways as you can: by email, through the postal service, by text, and phone. Post your thoughts on social media, but not in the way so many others do, in a constant tone of Really Angry. Helpful hints and reasonable ideas are better. Statements of concern can get through. One way or another, you can be heard. And even if you're not, you'll still be standing up for your beliefs. And you'll be actively engaged in a process that matters.

This all draws out something about the concept of voting in its broadest, and perhaps deepest, sense that a lot of the world seems not to understand. Many of our fellow citizens may not sufficiently have understood it, either. Real democratic voting is not just something that happens on a special day or a group of days set aside every year or couple of years. And it only occasionally involves polling places and ballot boxes. Everyday voting is something we do with our hands and feet, arms and legs, and hearts and minds on a daily basis. It's going on all around us, all the time. It happens in our homes. It takes place at work. It's a matter of the decisions we make as we determine what really counts, what's genuinely needed, and what's worth our full attention.

℘

*Ideas must work through the brains and the arms
of good and brave men, or they are no better than dreams.
Ralph Waldo Emerson*

℘

Voting every day is a matter of choosing to use our time, money, and resources in such a way as to support our country's founding values and our nation's health. It also means acting with the good of the world in mind. One of the great ironies in life is that a narrow selfishness in our actions is ultimately self-defeating. We've seen this play out in our economy on a broad scale. And we can witness it in people's lives around us as well. Criminals and the badly corrupt don't always get caught and punished by the legal system. But they do always get caught and punished by the spirit, as Socrates taught. Bad actions create worse people. Selfishness is ultimately self-destructive. A concern for the greater good, by contrast, most often secures our own good. We need to cultivate more responsible habits of thought and action focused on the greater good that will guide us to vote every day for things that matter. Then our true self-interest is helped, not harmed.

The area where I live had a water shortage. Everyone in the family had to monitor every bit of city water we used. We started taking quicker showers, putting less water in the tub, and not running the tap needlessly while brushing our teeth or shaving. My wife put a couple of large plastic garbage bins into service out back as water barrels to catch whatever rain we did sporadically get, which she could then use for our garden and plants. We developed a conservation mentality that led to positive new habits, and many of these routines have been continued since the shortage ended.

As concerned citizens, we need to be just as careful about electricity and gasoline, and various other petroleum based products, including plastics. We should seek to guard such important gifts of nature as our air, the topsoil, and our normal water sources. A deliberately cautious use of our limited resources is an act of patriotism. It's a way of voting every day. And a conservation mindset need not lead to outsized sacrifices that drastically reduce our quality of life. On the contrary, a conservation mentality can craft a lifestyle that's both enjoyable and sustainable, and one that will allow us all, as well as our descendants, to benefit from a better quality of life in the future.

ↄ

Great things are done by a series of small things brought together.
Vincent van Gogh

ↄ

Sometimes, simple sacrifice is necessary for long term good. Drive less. Carpool more. Use public transportation. Continue to employ virtual platforms for meetings when possible, and perhaps use them in more creative ways. Support small farms that have organic and sustainable practices. Eat responsibly. The thoughtful choices and minor sacrifices involved in a healthy and careful lifestyle need not diminish our ongoing experience in the least. They can in fact create the conditions of a better life for all of us who actually make those decisions to improve our behaviors.

It's been said recently that economic crises are hitting us now with increased frequency and intensity. There may be a parallel here between the economy and our ecology. Hurricanes, tornadoes, and other natural disasters are also happening with greater frequency and strength. And in both cases, the heightened storm activity may be coming, at least in part, from careless human action that feeds into complex systems we don't yet fully understand. Something similar could be said about most military actions of an offensive or aggressive form. They feed into complex systems we don't fully grasp, and so they almost never have the results expected. Much of human behavior confronts the famous law of unintended consequences for the exact same reason. As responsible and patriotic citizens, we need to be as careful with our economic choices as with our environmental conduct. We need to be cautious in our politics, and wary of charismatic firebrands who make complex issues sound simple and prefer to attack other people's approaches to the problems of our day rather than carefully and logically outlining their own. Bumper sticker wisdom isn't enough for a complex world. Grand gestures are sometimes needed in life. But the most good typically comes from small and reasonable improvements along the way.

Voting every day may mean changing our habits. It always means paying attention and taking positive action whenever we can. It could also sometimes involve recasting our commitments in major ways. I'm thinking of a young Ivy-league graduate who just left a good job in New York to enlist in the marines. I know an accountant and former corporate officer who joined the F.B.I. to make a bigger difference for our country. An old friend who works as an organizational consultant tells me he's recently had the time of his life as a volunteer scoutmaster. An accomplished woman in town successfully organized the funding and construction of a major new project for the community. Meanwhile, a busy neighbor has long voted with his time and energy to build up the local Boys and Girls Club, as well as other community organizations that support the many fundamental American values we hold dear.

❧

To make democracy work, we must be a nation
of participants, not simply observers.
Louis L'Amour

❧

These are people who vote every day. They give us examples
of patriotism we can believe in, an everyday patriotism in action.
Let's be counted among them. Let's join in their efforts for the
greater good and enjoy with them the quiet satisfaction that comes
from doing the right thing for our nation, often just by doing the
right thing for our neighbors, and making our best positive difference for the world around us whenever and wherever we can. We
don't have to quit our jobs or single handedly solve a major community problem through our efforts or leadership. We just have
to pay attention and seek to make a difference for the better from
addressing the needs we see around us.

Doing for others as we would like them to do for us, living out
the American dream based on the values of life, liberty, equality,
opportunity, justice, security, and service every day in our towns
and neighborhoods, in our volunteer organizations, in our schools
and our churches and synagogues and mosques will accomplish
great good, and send out an important signal. It won't be a message
as easily quantifiable as voter turnout on official election days, but
it will be one just as important for conveying our deep and genuine commitment to America, and through this nation to the best
hopes and dreams of the world.

The everyday patriot in our land is committed as a matter of
principle to the good of the entire international community. The
human family is a contentious bunch, as we certainly know. But
we all have the same ultimate origin and fundamental nature. The
Declaration of Independence, we should remember, says that *all*
men, in the inclusive sense of "human beings," are created equal,

not just those who happen to live within our borders. This great claim applies to everyone in Afghanistan, Iran, North Korea, Somalia, Ecuador, El Salvador, and any other part of the earth where, far too often, great numbers of little children have grown up without the most basic freedom and opportunity to become what they are capable of being. The values of our land can be a beacon in the night for all who aspire to the best that's possible in this life. We're just trying to do our part to blaze the way, clear a path, and help provide a greater measure of hope for the world, as well as for ourselves and our descendants in this land. Our small patriotic actions each day, as they accumulate and compound with the supporting efforts of others, can strengthen that hope for everyone.

No Time
for Cynics

As a nation, we've joked about politics and many of our politicians for a very long time. People have made careers out of poking fun at our elected representatives. And there's nothing wrong with that, done right. Laughter can be good, as long as mockery doesn't feed a false sense of ego, or improper superiority over others. Many of those we've chosen for political office in our history have given us plenty to laugh at. Humor can spark insight and be a powerful form of political commentary, or of dissent. Some of our elected representatives have made us mad, bewildered us, or just badly disappointed our hopes. Others have left us with something to regret and even grieve. But we don't have time right now to be cynical about our system, or despondently angry and fatalistically inert. That's not an indulgence we can afford. Our world is too challenging, and our nation needs us all as active participants in the process and adventure of America.

℘

Cynics are only happy in making the world as barren
for others as they have made it for themselves.
George Meredith.

℘

Perennial pessimists about government need to just get over their default settings of frustration, sarcasm, and righteous indignation. Not every politician is a crook. Not all lobbyists are liars. Government employees aren't divided into the three categories of mendacious felons, lazy shirkers, and incompetent fools. There are the wise and unwise in every job throughout the public and private sectors. And we actually know that. There is a distinction between reality and appearance in every walk of life. There are good and smart people holding things together in every facet of modern activity. Politics is no different. And it's unavoidably important, despite what the cynics may think or say.

Political leaders and government officials can make bad mistakes and create terrible harm when they ought to be solving problems and improving things. For many in our time, grandstanding has become a low performance art that eclipses any sense of responsibility for real governance. But I like to remind people of a philosophic principle I discovered long ago. I call it "The Double Power Principle." It says: For almost anything, whatever has great power for good tends to have equal and opposite power for harm; it's up to us how we use it. So, why do bad characters go into politics? It's at one level the same reason good people do: in the structures and processes of government, as in business, there is great power for making things happen. Great good or great harm can result. But if we vote everyday and in all official elections as we should, we can work to tilt the probabilities in favor of the good. No government official will ever be a flawless and perfectly wise solver of problems. But suitably wise and decent people at every governmental level can do good things, more often than not, that benefit us broadly.

The task of government, or the endeavor of governance, is simply a necessity at every level of our lives, and keeps chaos at bay. Plato's *Republic* may have been more about our souls than societies. In it, he indicated how we all have to govern our inner experience, emotions, and actions, as well as our households, commitments, and careers. To play on Plato and alter his famous quotation of Socrates, the ungoverned life is not worth living. Politics is just a way of serving our needs of governance at broader levels. Aristotle once said, "Man is a political animal," and he didn't mean to insult either us or the other animals. At its best, politics is life. It's the life of people together, adjudicating our differences, making acceptable compromises, tolerating, allowing, and affirming, seeking higher values, working out our hopes, and leaving our legacy to the future.

ᜒ

One of the penalties of refusing to participate in politics
is that you end up being governed by your inferiors.
Plato

ᜒ

A cynical or skeptical mindset about politics or life is a corrosive frivolity that won't help us now. In our high tech era, it's also a great and terrible danger. We can still be properly wary about any particular person who suddenly enters the political arena. We can and should question any new policy or program offered for our consideration. We can debate all issues of importance with feeling, and we ought to keep a close eye on all those who present themselves as championing our concerns. In fact, this is both our right and duty. As citizens, we should be carefully watchful over the common good. And it's only sensible to protect our own interests, wisely understood. But we need to put the posture of cynical disregard for all politics and politicians behind us.

For years, we've understood that healthcare isn't just the business of medical professionals. It's everybody's business. Environmental care is the same. And this is true of education, for obvious reasons. In a similar way, we need to realize just as fully that politics isn't just the business of professional politicians. It's your business and mine.

This is our country. It's time to reclaim it in all the right ways, not through angry rhetoric or intimidation, but through collaborative endeavors aimed at real goods. Let's take our cue and our motivation from the very idea of a Declaration of Independence. Let's declare our own personal independence from all forms of apathy, noninvolvement, and inertia. Let's put aside any lingering disdain for politics. Let's quit deriding politicians as a class and dismissing their intent. Let's raise the bar instead. Let's abandon any tactics of spreading fear and fury through exaggeration, caricature, and lies. Let's stop attacking each other. Let's conspire to leave conspiracy theories alone, and embrace productive ways of cultivating our gardens instead. By our positive attention and concern, we can make a real change, and we should, not simply because it's our duty, but also because it's our right. It's even an act of love, reflective of our highest values. It's in our interest to take action now to preserve, protect, and enhance our democracy together.

෴

What we need are critical lovers of America—patriots
who express their faith in their country by working to improve it.
Hubert H. Humphrey

෴

I don't think the founders of this country worked and fought for our freedom to have desperate slums, polluted cities, murdered children, mass incarceration, uneducated adults, legalized profiteering, political corruption, an outrage culture, homeless families, and shattered lives. They didn't yearn for a superficial throwaway society where inner growth is sacrificed to outer comfort and basic necessities are destroyed by reckless behavior. They wanted us to be a light to the world, not a stumbling block, a source of inspiration and hope, not a cause of resentment and hate. To the extent that we've diverged from their dreams, we have some serious work to do. And when we think of all those who have given their time, talents, and lives so that we might make good progress in attaining those dreams, we should be inspired to get busy in this work. Let's do what we can to see to it that no young patriot eager to serve in the defense of our country has ever sacrificed and struggled or perished in vain. We can help make those immense sacrifices count in our own day. It is up to each and every one of us to do our part.

Let's make our citizenship a positive, active reality in our lives. Let's show that patriotism is much more than waving a flag or singing the national anthem with gusto, or even pledging allegiance in a posture of respect. Let's honor the founders of this nation and our forebears and make them proud. Let's honor each other and make each other proud. Let's honor our children. Let's seek to make them and their children proud.

Putting Ideals
to Work

Winston Churchill is often reported to have observed that you can always depend on Americans to do the right thing, once they've exhausted every other possibility. And that's fine. We'll take the critique along with the compliment. This is indeed such a moment. We've tried nearly everything else. We know now what doesn't work. Torrents of abusive political rhetoric spewed out on television, radio, and across websites and social media outlets may in fact make their purveyors rich and play to the interests of our adversaries, but they do nothing but harm for our general polity and overall good. We need to turn away from all of that as a dangerous sideshow that will never lead us into the promised land that the divisive hawkers proclaim as the sure result of following them. Of course, it's really all about them. As ordinary citizens, we've tried leaving the business of America to other people, and we've learned some important lessons as a result. Now it's vital that we do the right thing, reawaken our attention, re-energize our actions, and refocus the concern that should never have faded in the first place. The business of America is indeed yours and mine.

I feel a new spirit just beginning to move across the land. Shock and anger are starting to give way to a heartfelt determination and a glimmering of hope. In less than a couple of decades, we've encountered the horrors of foreign terrorism on our soil, the most severe financial crisis since the Great Depression, unexpected spasms of deadly violence in public places, catastrophic weather events occurring with increased frequency, and a pandemic that as of this writing has killed over a million of our fellow citizens at nearly every age and in most walks of life. Foreign events concern us. And nobody can predict exactly what big problem we'll face next. But the worst that we can experience has always eventually brought out the best in us. The challenges from those who hate us, the scandals of all who would exploit us, the convulsions of our natural world, and the horrors of the furious and deranged have issued a wakeup call for us all. We have come to understand what we face, and we have begun to see more clearly the serious price of inaction. Television's Mr. Rogers long ago taught us to look for the helpers in times of trouble. Maybe it's time for us also to be those helpers. This is a chance for revival, a time to renew the true patriotic spirit of every man and woman and child in America. We all know we need it. Now, together, let's get busy and live it.

లా

The great end of life is not knowledge, but action.
T.H. Huxley

లా

I can feel the first stirrings of a healthy national rebirth and awakening focused on the values that lie behind the Declaration of Independence, our American Constitution in its entirety, the Gettysburg Address, Martin Luther King's moving orations, and all the many other great statements of national vision we've inherited from our rich and turbulent past. I see increasing numbers of people wanting to take action and make a difference with their lives. And I can see them beginning to do so in profound and practical new ways at the local Boys and Girls Club, through Habitat for Humanity, and in many other wonderful volunteer organizations that improve our communities.

I've personally experienced a great example of this close to home. A neighbor of mine was a founder of one of the top companies in its field globally. After helping to get the organization up and running, he wanted to take a break from the eighty hour weeks he had been working, and so he went off on what was supposed to be a short sabbatical, returning to his hometown of Wilmington, North Carolina for some much needed relaxation. A few months later, he heard about a cookie sale being held to help raise a million dollars for needed improvements to the local public library. Realizing that this would take more dough than the people involved had imagined, he envisioned a quicker path to the desired results and decided to help. In a very short time, a beautiful new branch of the library existed. In addition, this man of action was soon serving on several boards of local charitable organizations. As if this wasn't enough already, he had hatched the idea to start up an informal group of a novel sort, a civic endeavor in town that could make a difference to the community in a new and powerful way.

This innovative thinker and good neighbor invited me and one other friend to join him in bringing together two different groups of people in our southern coastal town, the old families who had lived here for generations and the recent transplants who have been moving in from all over the country and around the world. We would come together under a name connoting our unity, and we'd meet several times a year. The idea was that we'd be gathering for three reasons: charitable giving, relationship building, and personal education. Invited members would pay reasonable yearly dues that would be combined for targeted giving in the community, to meet local needs in an innovative way. We'd get to know each other across the divides of cultural heritage and experience, and we'd have luminary speakers to bring us information and wisdom from all sectors of modern life. Leaders in the community could share their various perspectives on pressing issues, and perhaps come up with new plans for how we could move forward in creative ways.

℃

A community is like a ship; everyone ought
to be prepared to take the helm.
Henrik Ibsen

℃

We recruited members quickly and brought together a group of accomplished people who were eager to make a difference. And good things happened right from the start. The public library, or the Boys and Girls Club, the pediatric wing of our hospital, the YWCA, or our town's fine art museum—one organization each year would be offered a single, large financial gift all at once, to make needed capital improvements or launch major new services they normally couldn't afford with the fragile nature of their ordinary operating budgets, most often based on unpredictable giving. Our combined resources could make a big difference to these important agencies and institutions that serve the overall good in our town and enhance our quality of life.

Local charitable organizations and community not-for-profits rarely know how and even whether badly needed funds will arrive, in even the best of economic times. The new group of assembled residents could, by their collective giving, offer these important groups a rare chance to know in advance that a major gift was coming all at once. Then they would have plenty of time to plan on how to use the money to do things that might not otherwise have been possible. In our case, thanks to the founder and his family, there were no administrative expenses for the group, so that all donated funds could go to whatever organization had been selected in a given year for this special help.

In addition to this distinctive mode of targeted giving, it was also determined from the outset that the group would have a strong social aspect. We began to assemble for a time of conversation and a long dinner three or four times a year to get to know each other, establish new friendships, and strengthen old ties. The seating arrangements would often introduce people who weren't previously acquainted, or at least didn't know each other well. The idea was that strong relationships can build strong communities. And it worked. My own charitable speaking as a philosopher was extended and enhanced through some of the relationships formed in those sessions.

It was also part of the founding vision of the group that there would be an educational and inspirational component to the meetings. At each dinner, we would have a speaker willing to donate his or her time to the cause—some active, creative, or very successful person from whose life and experiences we could learn. One of the top comics in America came and entertained us thoroughly. A man who had won the America's Cup Race more times than any other skipper in history visited from across the globe and spoke on what he'd learned about team excellence. We benefited from hearing best selling authors and top business builders who believed in this novel way of serving a community. A top presidential candidate even visited and kept asking me through the evening how in the world I manage to make a living as a philosopher. These guests made our times together even more interesting and always informative. And then, we'd often expand our circle of friendships to include the visiting speaker, to the greater good of all.

∽

Friendship is the only cement that will ever hold the world together.
Woodrow Wilson

∽

Thanks to a lot of creative initiative and hard work, this idea from one community member became a reality in all the intended ways, and the assembled group has been able to make a big difference in the lives of our neighbors. Each year since the creation of this enterprise, founding members have researched all the various needs in the area that have come to their attention, determined where the focused giving could make a difference, and then awarded a targeted contribution to the deserving recipient, watching carefully how the gift was used. Great things have happened as a result.

The group's existence and activities have strengthened the social and cultural fabric of the overall area in many ways. It's also been a lot of fun. All the members of the group have benefited from the experiences of getting together. And all have felt a deep sense of satisfaction in what the collective energy has been able to do. By giving a little money, some time, and a measure of attention to this original effort in community enhancement, many of us have broadened our vision of the area, connected up with great neighbors we hadn't previously known, and personally grown from all we've learned. The charitable giving at the core of the enterprise has been well directed, and it has been able to do many good things. I tell this story from my own personal experience just to indicate one of many creative ways we can get together to do good where we live, tending the garden we have.

❧

I deem it the duty of every man to devote a certain portion of his income for charitable purposes; and that it is his further duty to see it so applied as to do the most good of which it is capable.
This I believe to be best insured by keeping within the circle of his own inquiry and information the subjects of distress to whose relief his contributions should be applied.
Thomas Jefferson

❧

Anyone in America with vision, drive, and a commitment to serve can make a difference. Ten-year-old Talia Lehman sat at home several years ago in Des Moines, Iowa and watched the aftermath of Hurricane Katrina on television. She saw people suffering from the storm's devastation, and decided to do something about it. In a very short time she had organized other kids to "Trick-or-Treat" on Halloween for coins to fund a relief effort. Helped along by her parents and adult friends like Anne Ginther, who closed her own successful executive recruitment firm to become more involved in Talia's cause, they started a non-profit organization, Random-Kid, whose purpose was to assist young people in solving problems within their neighborhoods, their towns, our nation, and the world. Their motto was: "Any random kid can make a difference."

In a surprisingly short time, Talia and her new friends around the country helped raise over ten million dollars to contribute to the rebuilding of lives along the Gulf Coast through Habitat for Humanity and with other partner groups. And then they expanded their mission in many ways. Any young person aware of a real need could soon contact RandomKid through their website and get help in organizing a response.

I was fortunate to watch all this develop through reports from one of my old friends who served for a season on the board for RandomKid, due to the influence of his daughter, who as a teenager had gotten involved in their incredible activities. These efforts soon ranged from supporting hospitalized local children around the country to building a school in Cambodia, and providing well pumps for communities in Africa. Like the impulse behind any true act of concerned patriotic giving, the mission of RandomKid, which began on our soil, ultimately knew no borders.

You don't have to create a philanthropic group or join a charitable organization in order to do good for your community. You can get people together to pick up trash, fix an elderly neighbor's house, help a sick friend, clean up an empty lot, adopt a feral cat, cook for a family in need, or beautify a public space. Not all of us have money to give, but we all have time and energy. When people unite for a worthy cause, tremendous things can happen. This is the sort of active citizenship and everyday patriotism we can all believe in, a form of service embodied in ongoing concern and action for others.

っ

He who wishes to secure the good of others
has already secured his own.
Confucius

っ

I was talking not long ago to a great preschool director about a redistricting of public schools in our area. There was a new movement in our town and others to return to the concept of neighborhood schools. This would of course reverse decades of busing children to more distant locations for the worthy purpose of attaining healthier, diverse, and more equitable learning environments for all. But many school boards have been rethinking this long entrenched practice because of both economic and environmental concerns. Busing is expensive and it pollutes. In tight economic times, and with concerns for our environment mounting, the neighborhood school idea had come to appear more responsible and more sustainable on both these fronts to many local governments.

Parents also sensibly wanted their children closer to home during the day. Proximity allows easier access for family members and trusted neighbors in case of a child's sudden illness or any other emergency. It can also make volunteering more convenient for parents and other relatives. But of course, most neighborhoods around America still tend to lack the range of diversity we'd like to see in the classroom. For a variety of different reasons, people predominantly continue to live in neighborhoods that are in one or more ways homogeneous, whether socially, economically, or ethnically. This has some well-known and unfortunate side effects for neighborhood schools. Poor neighborhoods often have schools with poor outcomes. Affluent areas generally have schools that perform well. Students in both situations suffer from a lack of broadening contact with peers who have different lives and perspectives.

My teacher friend told me that many years ago she was an active member of the Parents and Teachers Association at a disadvantaged neighborhood school. When the PTA held a fundraiser to buy books for the library or musical instruments for the children, or to support an educational field trip, they might be able to raise a few hundred dollars, but it was always far short of the need. One PTA group she knew of at a wealthier school in the area could hold a fundraiser and bring in thousands of dollars, always equaling or exceeding their goals. She wrote to the prosperous PTA across town to ask if they would be interested in sharing some of their bounty with the less privileged students, and so investing in their communities and their children's larger environments in a new way. She told me she had never received a reply.

But that was then, as we like to say, and this is now. Hearing the story, it struck me that as citizens who care about our children, the future of our communities, and the overall prospects for our nation, we can't afford to let such extreme imbalances stand. If we really believe in such things as freedom, equality, opportunity, justice, and service, we need to take action to make sure that all our children have the fullest range of positive opportunities we can provide for good educations and a great start in life. If in fact neighborhood schools are coming back, then we should take action to remedy the unfortunate inequalities that still naturally result. The consequences affect us all. One PTA may not see it as a part of their mission. But other community groups might.

ᘏ

*The motivating force of the theory of a democratic way of life is still
a belief that as individuals we live cooperatively, and, to the best of
our ability, serve the community in which we live, and that our own
success, to be real, must contribute to the success of others.*
Eleanor Roosevelt

ᘏ

Parents at wealthier schools could take the initiative and reach out to a PTA group at a less advantaged school and form a partnership. Sister schools could engage in many forms of sharing through the year to enhance their students' experiences. One school might send their choral group or a dance team to perform at their partner institution. The other school could send their drama club to put on a play, or share a lively concert by their best musicians. There could also be mutual help in fundraising, involving an active participation in the process, and not just a sharing of results. There are so many possibilities for mutual enrichment between diverse schools. The exchange could be about much more than finances, and the overall relationship would then provide a context within which some form of fundraising sponsorship could have a more natural and organic role. Different neighborhood school communities could come to serve each other in many positive ways, and with the support of other groups.

We need to encourage creative thinking and innovative partnerships to address our local challenges and to make our own communities and our nation an increasingly better place. And that often requires breaking out of habitual patterns of thought and action. We all easily get trapped into routines of work and rest that keep us from even noticing things around us that need to be changed, or situations that could be improved. It's sometimes hard to venture out beyond the narrow circle of our typical daily concerns. We get in ruts. But by keeping our fundamental American values more in the forefront of consciousness, we may be more likely to spot things in our area or region, or even in the country, that are out of step with what we truly want and need. A new spirit of commitment can then make us more likely to do something creative about the problems we see. That can spark innovative partnerships or collaborations that may then go on to have even more benefits in unexpected ways.

℣

As long as habit and routine dictate the pattern of living,
new dimensions of the soul will not emerge.
Henry Van Dyke

℣

For decades, I've told friends that the worse things get, the more of an optimist I become. And that's because of a long established historical pattern. Something like the principle of entropy often seems to be at work on a social and existential level in the world. Untended, healthy situations tend to diminish and things fall apart. Weeds grow in the garden. Beautiful plants wither and die off. Because of a strange mechanism in human psychology, we can adjust to a gradual deterioration around us in such an unconscious way that we barely notice the issue. When things get sufficiently bad, though, we notice enough to complain. But out of habit, we typically do nothing more than comment and sigh, or grouse until things get so intolerably unacceptable that it's a wakeup call for everyone. Then we're finally motivated to get into gear and do something to make the changes that have long been needed. And the pendulum can begin to swing back.

I went to Russia with my family on a speaking trip right after the breakup of the Soviet Union. In the once beautiful city we visited, graffiti was everywhere and yards were overgrown with high grasses and weeds. Things were rusty, dirty, and neglected. There was blight so extensive that I thought it would be desperately hard to live with it every day. At a symphonic performance of transporting music, a stray dog walked across the stage in front of the large audience and scratched himself before lying down near the violins. The broader disorder had crept into the performance hall, but at least in a way that could cause a smile. I was reminded of places at home where things had gotten just as bad through a lack of attention over time. As a visitor, I was shocked by what I saw, but I had grown accustomed to similar sights in our land. We sometimes need the eyes of a tourist to see anew the things around us that have diminished and need to be restored.

In our time now, I can glimpse the first signs of a very positive swing of the social pendulum in our own nation, a rising tide of interest in community service and in righting some of the wrongs that have surfaced in recent years, after having been well hidden from many of us for quite a long time. And with our help, this can become a tide that will lift everyone up. One of the great lessons of life is that when we get involved in helping meet the needs of others in our communities, we end up indirectly benefiting ourselves as well. Ironically, individualism is not in our individual self-interest. It's the job of any citizen to look out for the overall good of our communities and to do what we can to improve them. As a result, we'll all have better places to live.

We can see the early indications of a wave of concern on the part of younger people, as well as many of their elders, for taking a more active role wherever they are, in matters of helpful service and creative community building. Though dampened a bit by the social restrictions and isolations required by our recent pandemic, I hear new voices refusing to accept an inertial slide any farther away from our principled ideals and founding values. And this social phenomenon seems to be growing. It's one of the great psychological laws of life that any positive action taken to solve a problem or meet a need will tend to attract to itself unanticipated help and resources.

I'm reminded of a letter that the great American Abigail Adams wrote to her husband, John, while he was away from home, working in Philadelphia during the year of 1776, trying hard to help establish the foundations of this country we enjoy and love. His days were arduous and often discouraging. Hope mingled with frustration as different voices from diverse parts of the land with conflicting interests struggled for recognition and even dominance in seemingly interminable meetings. Abigail wanted to encourage John to continue on and give his best to the enterprise. And so she decided to remind him about the larger importance of the moment. To do this, she quoted some of her favorite lines in Shakespeare, from a passage in the play "Julius Caesar" (Act 4, Scene iii) that reads, in full:

> There is a tide in the affairs of men,
> Which, taken at the flood, leads on to fortune;
> Omitted, all the voyage of their life
> Is bound in shallows and in miseries.
> On such a full sea are we now afloat,
> And we must take the current when it serves,
> Or lose our ventures.

Our moment, in its own distinctive way, is as fraught with insecurity, as chaotic, as important, and as full of possibility as theirs. And yet, we're beginning to experience some movement in the right direction. Let's take the clear positive current that we have right now, when it serves, and do something astonishing with it. Let's set out on this new rising tide, and sail on to a great destiny together. Let's take action and make our proper difference for each other, for America, and for the world that we are here to cultivate and enhance by doing our part as often as we can.

We should never be satisfied with anything less. Abigail Adams wasn't. And her husband John in the end wasn't either. He courageously persevered. And with his otherwise frequently squabbling colleagues, he set an extraordinary example and a suitably high standard in many ways for the rest of us.

ᔕᔓ

The conduct of our lives is the true mirror of our doctrine.
Montaigne

ᔕᔓ

Vote every day. Vote with your time, attention, and energy. Show the world what you think and believe in the best of ways. Demonstrate a commitment to your town and country. Be a great American in your own style and manner. Help a friend. Remain teachable. Listen with your heart to other perspectives. Do something good for somebody else. Check on a neighbor. Mentor someone. Give blood. And when your next Jury Duty notice arrives, don't suddenly become a Houdini of public service. Go do it well. Understand the importance of your time, attention, and service. Use your talents to make a difference for the greater good.

You can start small in showing your proper patriotism every day, or in raising its level a notch, but do indeed start. Take action, however great or small, and make the difference only you can make. The rest of us are counting on you. And you won't be in it alone. More of us than you might imagine will be doing it too.

The Declaration of Independence ends with the words, "We mutually pledge to each other our lives, our fortunes, and our sacred honor." Let's all of us make a mutual pledge in our own hearts to each other and our nation, today and every day we live.

Our Line
in the Sand

IN ONE OF THE MOST FAMOUS BATTLES fought in the course of American history—the Battle of the Alamo—at the end of a time of nearly constant bombardment, things suddenly grew quiet, nearly silent. Everyone was exhausted. The situation looked grim. Some who were present began pondering their dire prospects. The young attorney and commander of the Texas forces, Colonel William Travis, suddenly took out his sword and drew a line in the sand between himself and his remaining men. After explaining with great care the completely overwhelming odds they all faced at that moment, he said, "Those prepared to give their lives in freedom's cause, come over to me."

Instantly, all but one man stepped over the line. That lone individual remaining in place was the famous Jim Bowie, desperately sick with pneumonia and lying on a cot. He said, "Boys, carry me over," and at that moment crossed into history.

❦

The secret of man's being is not only to live
but to have something to live for.
Fyodor Dostoyevsky

❦

I don't have a sword today, and I can't draw a line in the sand for you, wherever you are in your life, and whatever you're doing. But I do have an urgent request. If you are prepared to give some of your time, attention, and talents to a great and crucial cause, and if you're willing to pledge a measure of your sacred honor to keep alive the hope of the world for such important values as life, liberty and the pursuit of happiness, please cross the starting line of active, energized citizenship and that exalted form of patriotism we can all believe in and live. Launch out onto the road of everyday patriotism that defines any great American, and make a lasting commitment today to do whatever you can to embody these sensibilities in your life. Find out right away how you can get more involved in your greater community, and then take new actions for the good of us all. Vote every day. The time is propitious. The opportunity is now. There is a tide. We can be the change we want to see in the world, for our day and beyond. Remember the Alamo and the commitments that were made there. Then go do what you can to perfect your little piece of the world. And in doing so, you will help to keep American ideals alive for the next generations to come.

Appendix One:

THE TOOLS OF SUCCESS

FOR MANY YEARS AS A PUBLIC PHILOSOPHER, I've been bringing people the tools of success that have been identified over the centuries by great thinkers who have lived before us. As I urge you to give your time and energy to projects that will benefit our communities and our nation, I thought it might be helpful to list briefly the seven most universal conditions of success passed on to us by wise people in the past. They can be found in the writings of many ancient practical philosophers, they crop up in nearly every century and culture, and can be glimpsed in the works of the quintessential American thinker, Ralph Waldo Emerson. They are developed at length in my own books *True Success* (1994) and *The Art of Achievement* (2002), as well as in *The Stoic Art of Living* (2004) and in some of the essays I post across social media on a regular basis. They're even positioned anew in one chapter of my recent book on how to deal with disruption and uncertainty, *Plato's Lemonade Stand: Stirring Change into Something Great*. More resources regarding these ideas also can be found at www.TomVMorris.com any time. Come visit online and use any of those resources to stimulate your own thoughts on what we most need right now.

From the times of ancient philosophy on through to the present day, the wisest diagnosticians of the human condition have specified that, for true success in any worthy endeavor, we need what I call The 7 Cs of Success:

1. A clear **CONCEPTION** of what we want, a vivid vision, a goal clearly imagined.
2. A strong **CONFIDENCE** that we can attain that goal.
3. A focused **CONCENTRATION** on what it takes to reach the goal.
4. A stubborn **CONSISTENCY** in pursuing our vision.
5. An emotional **COMMITMENT** to the importance of what we're doing.
6. A good **CHARACTER** to guide us and keep us on a proper course.
7. A **CAPACITY TO ENJOY** the process along the way.

Without a use of these tools, without action in conformity with these simple but powerful conditions, the best intentions may never translate into good results. With them, it's amazing what we can do. In fact, to see more about how we can form our inner lives so as to have greater results in the world as active citizens in our time, I hope you'll look for my short novel, *The Oasis Within*, available at www.TheOasisWithin.com or through the novels page on my website www.TomVMorris.com/novels. In a time when too many people operate in the one gear of "angry," it's possible to attain a measure of inner peace and power for achieving better results.

And I should mention one more thing. In a 1997 book entitled *If Aristotle Ran General Motors*, I suggested that there are four transcendental ideas that need to govern everything we do in our lives, communities, businesses, and in our national endeavors. My claim was that from the moment we wake up in the morning until the second we go to sleep at night, we experience the world along four dimensions, each of which has a target or foundation. They are (1) the intellectual dimension that aims at Truth, (2) the aesthetic dimension that aims at Beauty, (3) the moral dimension that aims at Goodness, and (4) the spiritual dimension that aims at a deep Unity, or connectedness. The best relationships, teams, companies, communities, and partnerships for the nation cannot arise well and fully flourish unless we always respect and nurture Truth, Beauty, Goodness, and Unity. I believe that as everyday patriots, we need to use these four great ideas as our guidance and guardrails in everything we do. We need to elect wise representatives and choose good leaders who value and live these four things, and we need to honor these values, or ideals, in all our words and actions.

Appendix Two

Little Things

Patriotism we can believe in, the patriotism of everyday life, is based on one important insight: Little things can have big results. When we vote every day with our time, attention, and efforts, we can make a real difference for our nation and our world. Don't overlook the small acts of citizenship and patriotic concern that are possible today while dreaming of a better America for us all tomorrow. You can take action now where you are. And you can make your mark for good. You might, for example:

- Mentor someone at work. Or befriend a younger person in your neighborhood.
- Smile at a policeman on duty or a security person in the airport, and say, "Thanks for being here."
- Coach or help out a kids' sports team or league. Encourage good sportsmanship.
- Volunteer to teach an adult class at church or in some other setting. Or just go.
- Attend a community meeting or the town hall discussion of a pressing issue.
- Shovel the snow off an elderly neighbor's drive or, depending on your part of the country, offer to mow a lawn, or haul away trash for someone who can't.

- Find a way to give an hour or two a week to some form of volunteer work.
- Read the Declaration of Independence and our Constitution. Maybe read some of it aloud to an older child. Talk with a young person about our democracy.
- Encourage a child to read a short, age appropriate book on the founding of our country, or on some of the characters involved in it.
- Help in a political campaign, in however small a role.
- Write a positive note to an elected official praising him or her for something you personally appreciate. That will certainly get some attention. And it will be valued.
- When the local fire department or high school or VFW chapter has a fish fry or cookout for fund raising, go eat and have some fun. Talk to someone there you don't know.
- Write a constructive letter to the editor of your local paper on some issue or story you care about. And try to be positive.
- Read a book now and then on something related to the history or functioning of our country, and talk to someone about what you've read.
- When you notice a problem, try to get involved in a solution.
- Whenever you hear angry, crass, and unfair political discourse on television or the radio, or online, turn it off. When you see it on social media, don't engage. Let it go. When you hear such ugliness in person, do what you can to diplomatically discourage this generally unhelpful approach to politics, and try to steer the conversation in a more positive direction. If more of us did this, we'd have a more civil society and perhaps politics could become a bit more about statesmanship than gamesmanship.

Appendix Three

COMMON SENSE

IN 1774, BENJAMIN FRANKLIN helped a young man emigrate from England to America. In his home country, Thomas Paine had experienced a series of business and personal failures, but he apparently had a sharp mind, and when he met Franklin, the prominent American suspected that young Thomas could get a new start in the colonies and make his mark here. In a fairly short time and after a very difficult voyage, Paine arrived in Philadelphia and soon got involved in writing magazine essays about the political situation of the day, urging his fellow colonists to come together and break from England, where he had experienced such dismal fortunes, and set up their own sovereign nation. He wrote a small book called *Common Sense* that was quickly bought and read by a broad segment of society at the time, and it became one of the best selling books in American history. When the book was published in January of 1776, serious troubles had already begun between the American colonies and the British homeland. Most people wanted some form of reconciliation with England, but Paine argued vigorously for revolution instead.

In our time, we clearly need a different revolution, one against destructive partisanship and the growing threat of authoritarianism, one of reconciliation with each other for the sake of our present and future progress. Though Thomas Paine was apparently a difficult person, later in life proving the appropriateness of his last name, some of the words in his small famous book are surprisingly timely. They reverberate in our present day and are worth quoting here as a reminder that, periodically, we need to revive and renew a proper spirit in our nation in order to chart forward an appropriate and healthy future together. Here are a few short passages from his booklet, easily available online, with the now standard paragraph numbers for reference.

> *The cause of America is in a great measure the cause of all mankind. (4)*

> *In the following pages I offer nothing more than simple facts, plain arguments, and common sense: and have no other preliminaries to settle with the reader than that he will divest himself of prejudice and prepossession, and suffer his reason and his feelings to determine for themselves: that he will put on, or rather that he will not put off, the true character of a man, and generously enlarge his views beyond the present day. (55)*

> *The sun never shined on a cause of greater worth. 'Tis not the affair of a city, a county, a province, or a kingdom, but of a continent—of at least one eighth part of the habitable globe. 'Tis not the concern of a day, a year, or an age; posterity are virtually involved in the contest, and will be more or less affected, even to the end of time, by the proceedings now. Now is the seed time of continental union, faith and honor. The least fracture now will be like a name engraved with the point of a pin on the tender rind of a young oak; the wound will enlarge with the tree, and posterity read it in full grown characters. (58)*

We ought not now to be debating whether we shall be inde-
pendent or not, but anxious to accomplish it on a firm, secure,
and honorable basis, and uneasy rather that it is not yet began
upon. Every day convinces us of its necessity. (162)

WHEREFORE, instead of gazing at each other with suspi-
cious or doubtful curiosity, let each of us hold out to his neigh-
bor the hearty hand of friendship and unite in drawing a line
which, like an act of oblivion, shall bury in forgetfulness every
former dissension. Let the names of Whig and Tory be extinct;
and let none other be heard among us than those of a good cit-
izen, an open and resolute friend, and a virtuous supporter of
the RIGHTS of MANKIND and of the FREE AND INDE-
PENDENT STATES OF AMERICA. (164)

Paine gives us a rousing end to his booklet and a great call to
action that is as applicable to our time as it was to his. And as the
French political genius Alexis de Tocqueville said in his later mas-
sive study *Democracy in America,* whose first volume appeared in
1835, a work that has been characterized both as the best book ever
written about democracy and also as the best ever written about
America:

Democracy does not give the most skillful government to the
people, but it does what the most skillful government is often
powerless to create; it spreads a restive activity through the
whole social body, a superabundant force, an energy that nev-
er exists without it, and which, however little circumstances
may be favorable, can bring forth marvels. (Volume One, Part
Two, Chapter Six)

Perhaps we can together rise to the occasion and bring forth
marvels in our own time.

Acknowledgements

I'd like to thank all the friends and colleagues who took time out of their busy schedules to read early drafts of this little book for its original first edition, which was very different from this version in many ways, and they responded whenever I needed a quick opinion, encouraged me in its publication, and contributed in various ways to its final form. Those who gave especially extensive attention to earlier stages of the book and provided helpful comments for its improvement included Dave Baggett, Dave Phillips, Jerry Walls, Mim Harrison, Peter Osborne, Mary Yorke, Scott Whisnant, and my wife Mary Morris. I owe them a lot. Thanks especially to Mike Priddy, who put three thousand copies of the original into the hands of people who could use it, and then more recently encouraged me to consider this all-new edition of the book for our time. Dr. Bruce May, going strong in his nineties, gave a careful reading to the manuscript and made many helpful suggestions along the way. He was also a real encouragement to me during this project. He's an example of a great American and everyday patriot, still working hard to help improve his community and his world. Thanks also to my old friend Norman, who is about to turn one hundred years old as I write these words, and whose phone call one day sparked the ideas that would lead to this little book. I also want to express my deep appreciation to the thousands of other individuals who read an earlier version of this, written for a very different time, and whose keen interest goaded me to continue to think about these issues and make this little manifesto right for our time now, and to make it also more public.

Dave Baggett, Mike Priddy, Joey Dumont, Steve Coggins, Willow Cheong Yang Taylor, Michael Bossone, Aaron Simmons, Michael Barnwell, Tim Brown, Jack Malcolm, and Mark Boundy have also offered detailed comments on a previous draft of this edition, and helped me immensely to improve it. I thank them for their ideas during a busy time.

I want to express my gratitude in advance to anyone who reads this book and takes action on its simple recommendations. Thank you for helping to make our nation better and stronger for all our children, including mine, and also for my wonderful granddaughter, Grayson. They deserve the best we can give them. I also want to thank all the great Americans I know in every walk of life who have inspired me to believe that, in this amazing country, and in our world, despite any appearances that we may face to the contrary, positive change can happen, and so the best is yet to come.

No act of kindness, however small, is ever wasted.
Aesop

About the Author

A native of North Carolina, Tom Morris was a Morehead Scholar at The University of North Carolina (Chapel Hill), now the Morehead-Cain, and has been honored as a recipient of their "Distinguished Young Alumnus Award." He holds a Ph.D. in both Philosophy and Religious Studies from Yale University, and for fifteen years served as a Professor of Philosophy at the University of Notre Dame. He quickly went on to become one of the world's most active public philosophers, speaking to groups all across America and around the globe. Tom's philosophical work has been supported in the past by the National Endowment for the Humanities and The George A. and Eliza Gardner Howard Foundation at Brown University. He also holds honorary doctorates of humanities and letters in recognition of his work. Tom can be contacted any time through his website, www.TomVMorris.com.

After a number of books published by Oxford, Cornell, and Notre Dame, among other academic publishers, Tom's popular book, *True Success: A New Philosophy of Excellence*, launched him into a new adventure as a public philosopher. His philosophical audiences have included a great number of the largest companies and trade associations in the nation and around the world.

Tom is also the author of the highly acclaimed business best-seller, *If Aristotle Ran General Motors,* and the even more recent big yellow book often seen in college dorms nationwide the night before final exams, *Philosophy for Dummies.* His other books include *The Art of Achievement, The Stoic Art of Living, If Harry Potter Ran General Electric, Socrates in Silicon Valley,* and *Super-heroes and Philosophy,* where Superman and Batman finally meet Plato and Aristotle. His newest book on transformational action in the face of difficulty challenges is entitled *Plato's Lemonade Stand: Stirring Change into Something Great.*

Tom is now also a novelist, having published *The Oasis With-in,* a little book many are comparing to *The Alchemist* and *The Little Prince,* among other small modern classics. This is a short prologue to a new series of action, adventure, and philosophical fiction wisdom books set in Egypt in 1934 and 1935, collectively entitled "Walid and the Mysteries of Phi." Its first volume, *The Golden Palace* has launched a new way of doing philosophy, fol-lowed up in all subsequent volumes, as described at the website, www.TheOasisWithin.com.

Tom's work has been covered by such diverse news media as CNN, CNBC, NBC, NPR, *The New York Times, Fast Company, The New York Times Magazine, USA Today, Newsweek, The Los Angeles Times,* the *Chicago Tribune, USA Weekly, The Economist, Readers' Digest,* German *Elle, Die Zeit,* and many other magazines and newspapers around the world. He is a proud American and avid citizen of the world. Through books, essays, an active online presence and over twelve hundred public talks, his message is help-ing to change lives and revolutionize business practices everywhere.

I am a citizen of the world.
Diogenes